Building
High Commitment
in a
Low-Commitment World

Other Books by Bill Hull

Can We Save the Evangelical Church?
The Disciple-Making Pastor
The Disciple-Making Church
Jesus Christ, Disciple Maker

Building
High Commitment
in a
Low-Commitment World

Bill Hull

Fleming H. Revell
A Division of Baker Book House Co
Grand Rapids, Michigan 49516

Published by Fleming H. Revell
a division of Baker Book House Company
P.O. Box 6287, Grand Rapids, MI 49516-6287

Paperback edition published 1997

Printed in the United States of America

Library of Congress Cataloging-in-Publication Data

Hull, Bill, 1946–
      Building high commitment in a low-commitment world / Bill
Hull.
            p.   cm.
      Includes bibliographical references.
      ISBN 0-8007-1711-2 (cloth)
      ISBN 0-8007-5633-9 (paper)
      1. Commitment to the church. I. Title.
BV4520.H779 1995
248.4—dc20   95-9142

Contents

Introduction   7

Part I   **The Struggle for Commitment**
   1. What Makes It So Difficult   13
   2. Our Evangelical Mythology   23
   3. Three Myths about Commitment   31
   4. The Top Ten Enemies of Building High
      Commitment   49

Part II   **Reasons to Be Committed**
   5. People Need Big Reasons   81
   6. Ten Disciplines of the Committed
      Christian   95
   7. The Fulfilled Life   117

Part III   **How to Build and Keep Commitment**
   8. Seven Steps That Build High Commitment   127
   9. Three Steps That Maintain Commitment   165

   Notes   201

Introduction

Can a person be a good Christian and not be highly committed to Christ and his church?

NO!

There, I said it!

However, if you cross out *good*, you could say it *is* possible for a person to be a mediocre, disobedient, lousy, stagnant Christian and not be committed to Christ and his church.

Contemporary evangelicalism has made a god in its own image. That god is relevant and user-friendly. You might say that it's a designer god. Look at the god of contemporary evangelicalism, and you don't see red; you don't see the shed blood that cleanses us from all our sin. Instead, color this idol mauve, the trendy color found in most upscale restaurants.

As an alternative to the designer god's claims, I propose that we allow Jesus to define the normal Christian experience. Even a cursory reading of Scripture shows that Jesus defined normal Christianity as requiring a high commitment on the part of the average disciple. Therefore I must ask, "If being tepid is abnormal and substandard by Jesus' definition, why do many Christian leaders tell consumer-oriented disciples that it's okay to be that way?"

The enemy that keeps the church from reaping a great harvest comes from within. Attempts to make it more relevant and user-friendly at the expense of its discipline and health seriously weaken the church. On top of this, moral relativism and materialism have gradually seduced the church, shredding its integrity.

The highly prized cutting edge on which many leaders want to live turns out to be a treacherous cliff over which many have already fallen. The move away from submission to spiritual authority and the disciplined life is at the root of the deteriorating health of many congregations. As our leaders madly rush toward the relevant and what works, many have taken their eyes off the task of building healthy Christians who will reach others where they live, work, and play. The huge overbalance of the "on campus" ministries of the church and the malignant neglect of "off campus" outreach is merely a symptom of our retreat from the normal Christian life.

> Do not be deceived: God cannot be mocked. A man reaps what he sows. The one who sows to please his sinful nature, from that nature will reap destruction; the one who sows to please the Spirit, from the Spirit will reap eternal life. *Let us not become weary in doing good, for at the proper time we will reap a harvest if we do not give up.*
>
> Galatians 6:6–9, italics added

By accepting substandard Christianity as normal, we have practiced sowing to the flesh. There is no possibility that an undisciplined follower of Christ who is not practicing the spiritual disciplines and doing so with perseverance can please God or reap the harvest that God intended for him and the church. We must learn to define normal Christianity as God defines it. Pastors and Christian leaders must call the church to normality and create structures and accountability to make it a reality before we can experience the great harvest.

It's time to stop blaming the media, the liberals, the National Organization for Women, the American Civil Liberties Union, and our dysfunctional pasts. Let's start searching our own souls.

My purpose in this book is

1. To present high commitment as the normal Christian life.
2. To expose the existing evangelical ethos as abnormal and substandard.
3. To raise the commitment level of the church by convincing leaders that we have been seduced into the acceptance of mediocrity as normal.
4. To give some clear steps that will build high commitment and help people keep their commitments.

Simply stated, this book is a call back to the normal Christian life.

Part I

The Struggle for Commitment

1

What Makes It So Difficult

The contemporary evangelical church environment works against high commitment. Fully committed Christians are considered a bit hyperactive, monastic, and let's admit it, they're labeled odd. "No one needs to eat and sleep religion" goes the lament.

At times, people might honor a committed Christian's dedication, but the prevailing view is that such a life is not practical. Not only that, a committed lifestyle is not seriously pursued because the general church environment does not require it for acceptance or leadership.

That has led the luminous Bill Hybels to conclude, "Becoming totally devoted to Christ is the most difficult single topic to get across to people. When I teach this to secular minded people, they think I'm from Mars."[1]

Hybels is not alone: A great company of pastors and leaders confront the same response. But there is a huge difference between those who teach high commitment as normal and believe it and those who teach it but don't believe that it is normal. Those who believe might not expect much, but at least they have an optimistic starting point. Those who believe high commitment is not the norm will find it rare indeed.

If leaders want to experience the high-commitment society in our low-commitment world, they must begin by believing their own theology. If you think that the Bible teaches high commitment as normal and all else as inferior, then there is hope that the church will experience the reality of teamwork espoused by 1 Corinthians 12:12–13 and Ephesians 4:11–16. With that kind of teamwork, a congregation could become a meaningful participant in the Great Commission.

The Emotional Journey

Most pastors and church leaders I know have locked horns with the prevailing culture and honestly struggle to build high commitment. Admittedly, it *is* a struggle. I am presently engaged in helping train thousands of church leaders. They experience no greater challenge or frustration than to consider high commitment as the norm and attempt to communicate it and make it happen.

At one time leading others into high commitment was extremely frustrating for me. My frustration would build over a period of four to six weeks. Only a few members would give 10 percent to the church; fewer would want to engage in evangelism; a minority regularly read the Bible or prayed. Yet everyone wanted a full-service church without supporting it either in money or time. Eventually I would spew my angst upon the congregation.

As pastor, I found it easy to be seduced by a spiritual superiority complex and to project my "righteous anger" onto unsuspecting saints. This led to periodic "van Gogh" type tirades, in which I ranted and raved concerning the deplorable state of our commitment level—without cutting off my ear. (Some suggested my tongue as an alternative.) On one occasion I reached an emotional crescendo and screamed (or prophetically held forth), "If you are as tired of playing church as I am, meet me at two o'clock this afternoon, and we will go door to door in this community and reach some people for Christ."

One person stood to her feet and with great feeling said, "Yes."

I responded, "Sit down, honey."

(The last part isn't true. No one stood, *especially* not my wife, who would rather have a tooth extracted than do door-to-door witnessing.)

It was a cathartic moment for me. I felt better, but I was the only one; nothing was accomplished.

"The advantage of the emotions," wrote British playwright and gadfly Oscar Wilde, "is that they lead us astray." This is so true, particularly for spiritual leaders, because our work is wrapped in emotion. The unreliable nature of the emotions often causes us to draw a series of interesting conclusions. We start feeling that the people we work with are carnal; they are fakes, phonies. We each think, *If only I had spiritual people like myself, I could really do something.* Translation: "If they would like what I like and do what I tell them, this church would grow, and I would look good and feel better about myself."

Of course, a leader may have other emotional reactions instead. He may think: *I'm no leader. God didn't call me. How could I have been so wrong? How can I ever again have confidence that God is speaking to me?* Or he might turn against his congregation, thinking, *They are lukewarm; God will spew them out of his mouth, and so will I.* Another might feel, *These are the last days. The spirit of the age has them by the throat; they are disciples of their culture.* Or perhaps one might say, "We've all been mugged by the world, the flesh, and the devil."

Most leaders feel and must deal with this kaleidoscope of emotion. It lies at the core of the struggle.

The Philosophic Journey

"To thine own self be true" is the axiom our contemporary culture has adopted. In fact, the updated version seems to be: "To thine own self be dedicated. Be fulfilled, regardless of what is true, because truth is what makes you feel good."

One of contemporary society's most revered skills is the ability to create one's own version of the truth. America is thoroughly psychologized, and almost everyone has mastered the nomenclature of self-fulfillment. People are in a mad search for self, for warmth, for the designer lifestyle, tailored just for them. Instead of "do unto others as you would have them do unto you," it is "get your own needs met first." Until you have made that fascinating trip to find yourself, to find the "real me," you can't do anything meaningful in life. The prevailing culture is one huge therapy session. Our country's president claims to "feel our pain." He is just one among the high priesthood of self-proclaimed therapists. With the advent of television our culture now uses drama instead of reason to make its point. Impact is paramount; truth has become an orphan looking for a home, a place of residence in the available cleavages of the national psyche.

The philosopher Goethe wrote, "Ages which are regressive and in process of dissolution are always subjective, whereas the trend in all progressive epochs is objective." Because we are living in a subjective, therapeutic age, we are faced with several secondary barriers that make building high commitment harder.

Let me list two barriers for you:

The Elevation of Choice. Life is a menu; choose what you want, says today's world. The more affluent a society, the bigger the menu. Life in Western culture is like a restaurant with a menu so long that patrons need twenty minutes to read it. The dual increase of information and available products has made life more complex and more stressful.

In a free society, choice has always meant that a person can decide what religion, place of residence, or job he would like to have. He can support the politician and football team of his choice. Though I'm not denying the importance of choice in our society, today it has taken on a new quality. Elevated from an opportunity to a moral value, choice has taken its place in the pantheon beside moral virtues such as the Ten Commandments. In some cases it sits alone at the top of all moral good. For example, the taking of an innocent life through abortion is permitted, based on the highest moral value of choice. Choice overrules the prohibition of murder. When unmarried people choose to live together, choice overrules the prohibition of premarital or extramarital sex.

Though one would like to think that this kind of foolishness would not dupe the average Christian, that would be a false conclusion. Many churchgoers have adopted this thinking as wholeheartedly as secularists have, resulting in a consumer mentality on the part of the average churchgoer. The church is a salad bar, according to this philosophy. Take what you want; leave what doesn't look good.

Conditioned by this powerful cultural force, people think of shorter and lighter commitments. Another manifestation of the same philosophy simply proclaims, Don't commit yourself, because you might miss an unforeseen opportunity to do something else tomorrow. Led by such responses, many church leaders have begun to think, *People won't make commitments anymore, so why try?*

If Christians will not make commitments, then high commitment as a norm is out and accommodation to culture is in. Leaders often dismiss the idea that the church can be what it should be, and collecting large amounts of semicommitted underachievers becomes the norm.

It has always been difficult to argue with success, especially in the United States. After all, how can you object to the growing number of bodies, bucks, and buildings, when it's all accomplished in the name of God? Under this philosophy, challenges to conventional church success become almost heresy. Slaying the powerful philosophic mores of our superficial pop culture has become a challenge fit for a giant killer.

The Entitlement Mentality. Today's American feels entitled to have the best of everything. You experience that attitude when you hear statements such as:

> "The government owes me."
> "I deserve a break today."
> "Every person has a right."
> "I'm looking for a church that can meet my needs."

In politics the entitlement mentality is on the loose, and no one has a leash. Politicians promise to cut the deficit and balance the federal budget. Many make sincere promises, but they soon become aware that it requires the collective will of Congress to accomplish their objective. The fly in the ointment is the powerful lobbies that say, "You can cut the budget as long as it doesn't hurt our constituencies." Self-interest overpowers doing the right thing or taking the action that in the long run is in our best interest.

In the church this same spirit manifests itself in the great evangelical adventure, "looking for the church God has for us" or "shopping for a church." I am all for people prayerfully attempting to locate the best church for them. However, I believe the decision should be a bit different from choosing your entrée at a cafeteria. When I was a pastor, I was frequently asked, "What will your church do for me?" "How do you plan to keep my son safe from evil?" "Will we feel good here?" "Is there spiritual warmth?" "I won't have to work too hard, give too much, or feel uncomfortable, will I?"

My Kids Deserve the Best. How many families have decided whether or not to attend a church solely on the existence of a youth program that will meet the needs of their children? Many a frustrated small church pastor has lost good people who like everything about his church and could make a valuable contribution. Yet they choose a larger church with a full-time youth minister or exciting appendage. The question that freezes most pastors in their tracks is "Shouldn't my kids come first? I only have them for a short time, and in days like these, they need every help we can get to keep them with the Lord."

I would answer *no!* My kids don't come first; my family does. The most important factor in a child's spiritual development is the parents' spiritual development. Peer relationships are important and so are alternative social and recreational opportunities to counteract the secular options. But it is absolutely foolish for parents to sacrifice their opportunity and challenge to grow just for a youth program that appears to be better.

The "best" may mean pioneering a youth work. Churches across America desperately need a family or two to say, "We will take on the task of starting a healthy youth work." This actually has much more potential to build teens' Christian character than the majority of self-serving, fun-oriented youth works.

In many cases church choice means simply doing what the kids want. That is no way to run a family, make decisions, or train children. Looking for the full-service youth program that appears to be the most fun is part of the entitlement mentality that has thoroughly saturated our evangelical church culture. It is quite rare to find a family or person who approaches the church asking, "How can I serve? What can I do to help?"

I Deserve the Best. You don't have to have teens to be swept up in the entitlement attitude. Entitlement comes wrapped in many packages, and leaders need to watch out for people who want "only the best for the church"—on their own terms.

Immediately after the service he greeted me and thanked me for my faithfulness to the Word. This is usually the underhanded kind of complement reserved for a moment in which the hearer reaches back into his creative Rolodex in obedience to the axiom "If you can't say something nice, don't say anything." Even "wet behind the ears" pastors learn to recognize such faint praise. Within five minutes I knew he was wealthy, personally friendly with at least ten well-known evangelical luminaries, and accustomed to power, prestige, and getting his own way. I also picked up a strong whiff of condescension; I knew I was in for an interesting experience. Our church had been chosen by God to receive many blessings from this wise and wealthy sage, but for the many blessings we were about to receive, he expected something in return. I guessed the price tag read "position, prestige, and obedience to his suggestions." I wasn't sure how it would happen, but I knew it would.

On a Tuesday evening I was to have dinner with our Newcomers Class. For five weeks a gifted layman had led the group. On week six I was asked to join them for dinner and answer questions. After dinner we retired to the family room for a time of interaction. This was the time for our new member to administer his first real dose of the prescription medication that would cure our ills. A list unrolled from his hand and descended three feet to the floor below. Then for over one hour he proceeded to critique everything from hymn selection to sermon illustrations. We discussed so many of our shortcomings that space and my ego will not permit further expansion. Obviously he had bent many a pastor over a barrel.

After completing his list, he asked, "Well, Bill, what do you suggest I do?" In other words, "If you want me and my money and influence in your church, how many of these suggestions are you going to heed?"

I answered, "I suggest you find another church that will meet your needs. Obviously we have failed to do so." Our church wasn't for sale, and neither was I.

Our culture has spawned too many who believe they deserve the best for their time, effort, and money. In contrast, I believe the Scriptures show that we should humbly receive whatever God has given to us and jump at the opportunity to serve. And we should do it with the attitude that serving isn't a right, but a privilege—it is an honor to be part of what God is doing. One can only wish that evangelicals would consult with God as much on leaving churches as on joining them. If such care is exercised in discerning his will to join, shouldn't equal attention be given to the decision to exit a ministry?

Doubtless, culture has discipled many contemporary Christians, and this has dampened church leaders' optimism regarding achievement of high commitment in their congregations. But God has not given us a spirit of defeat. Instead he's provided us with the power to kill the giant, if we will only commit ourselves to the task.

2

Our Evangelical Mythology

The New Priesthood

Os Guinness first called evangelical megachurch pastors and pundits the new priesthood. They have replaced theologians and denominational presidents as "when they speak, we listen" types.

Because they have produced what all others desire and respect—culturally relevant, big evangelical churches—megachurch pastors are heeded and given the immediate respect of colleagues, business leaders, and religion editors. They have created ministries that meet the contemporary evangelical "truth test": If it works, it must be right.

Contemporary evangelical "street level" theology is pragmatic to the core. To most, it makes little difference if the church has grown based upon a diminished gospel that does not require repentance or obedience or discipline. If challenged, pragmatists drive a stake through your heart with, "What kind of growth are you experiencing?" or, "How many have you reached?" These are good questions, and for many of us, require serious reflection. But in this

23

case the questions are accusations that imply the ultimate good is growth.

Most megachurch pastors are very gracious and would not ask the above questions. Generally these leaders are not the problem. In fact, to help struggling pastors, they teach seminars that provide useful information.

The problem starts when people try to copy the megachurch leaders. In their mad dash for success, leaders who emulate megachurch pastors often fall into patterns as contorted and useless as those of an Elvis impersonator. People don't know if they should laugh or cry at such attempts; they only know that this is not the real thing.

The problem is that, for many, the new priesthood's teaching seems to transcend all other information, including Scripture. Though the megachurch pastor may not teach anything antiscriptural, a student may rush to practice a method that violates who he is, who his congregation is, and what Scripture teaches concerning development of people.

Wading-Pool Theology

An example of contemporary pragmatic theology that many teach as the way to reach large groups of people is what I call "wading-pool theology." This belief says that entry-level commitment must be shallow at first. A simple knee-deep commitment is all people will make. I happen to agree with this concept as it relates to newcomers and seekers. However, the problem arises when such a low-level, user-friendly approach is extended to the continuation of the Christian experience. The Scriptures teach that all should graduate from the wading pool to the Olympic pool. All must engage in the challenge of learning new and difficult strokes, like the butterfly or breaststroke. Diving from various heights and learning twists and turns with varying degrees of difficulty should be a normal experience.

In contrast to the scriptural paradigm, much of contemporary teaching places the premium on gathering people and multiplying the wading-pool level experience. Many fast-growing churches' small-group systems neglect the need for spiritual growth and development. Leaders in these congregations believe in monolithic low-level groups that expand quickly, and for that to take place, the commitment level will be low.

Contrary to popular belief, most groups settle at the level of the weakest members, rather than the highest. This may be done under the banner of love, in order to make the least committed members feel cared for and accepted. The answer to such a problem is a progressive small-group system that gradually increases the requirements so that people will develop their spiritual strength. Whether or not we say that it is not our goal to leave people at the wading-pool level, very few will leave it unless we design a system that challenges them and establishes intentional progress.

If a very successful pastor says that people won't make high and long commitments anymore, he is wrong. He is filtering his opinions through his charismatic personality and experience. His church has grown because of his ability to connect with and inspire the masses, and gifted leaders usually undervalue the importance of their own gifts. It is more flattering and comforting to think that success results from new and innovative thinking rather than from the power of personality and leadership.

If a successful leader suggests that seekers don't want to feel guilty so you shouldn't talk about sin and the need for repentance, his advice shouldn't successfully pass through your theological gauntlet.

Beware: Pundits Disguised as Prophets

I know how treacherous and fragile are the prognostications of a pundit, for I am one. A pundit is anyone with influence who gets a forum in which to express an opinion. That's why actors can pontificate concerning serious political issues about which they know very little. From their multilevel homes in Beverly Hills they lament over the poor, and from the ski slopes of Vail they scold the military for bombing tyrants. Columnists, commentators, and reporters are frequently more famous and make more money than those about whom they report, so they have the power and the opportunity to control and shape public opinion. Athlete domination of both the broadcast booth and advertising industry has given them many opportunities to expound on a variety of subjects on which they know very little. Fame has become the coin of everyday exchange. Regardless of their origin, the culture of celebrity permits such philosophical lightweights to make a heavy impact.

Once again the evangelical community has not escaped such deleterious thinking. On occasion we get lucky. Chuck Colson was struck with fame (or infamy) by his participation in the Watergate scandal. The personal crisis in Colson's life led to his conversion to Christ and subsequently to his spectacular contribution to the church. In our culture there is no greater spokesman for Christ than Chuck Colson. But do you think that we would even know his name at all if he had been working at the Waterloo City Hall as city controller and was caught with his hand in the till? His fame originated in the position he held before conversion and was rooted in his secular success rather than in theological training or achievement. As Colson studied Scripture, learned from mentors like R. C. Sproul, and chose a difficult ministry to prisoners, he grew into an eloquent spokesman for Christ. For every Colson, however, there are many others who simply "spout off" without credibility.

Machismo and Money

There are two quick and easy roads to the world of evangelical punditry. The first is to be good at any sport, and the second to be successful at almost any business. Who is against great athletes and outstanding business leaders? Not me! I admire both and find them interesting and engaging people. The difficulty comes when a person with either background becomes a Christian, and Christians find out. Experienced Christians who should know better are quick to exploit these celebrities for the achievement of their own goals. Usually it starts with a testimony. Normally this is helpful, and no one gets hurt; even if the gospel is presented in an incomplete or misleading way, one can always say that a positive influence for Christ was left with the hearers. However, Christian celebrities often present a very soft gospel that leaves out sin, repentance, and the need for a real change. Often the pragmatic, "try it, you'll like it" message implies that if it doesn't work for you, you can always discard it.

A greater problem ensues when the untrained and often inconsistent-living celebrity grows in influence and writes his or her first book (usually a biography that's had a lot of help from a ghostwriter). In it the celebrity proposes his or her own brand of theology, and the influence is far out of proportion to its value.

Statistical Punditry

A new breed of prophet in the contemporary church is a guru with a pocket protector, who believes that "hard data" is essential to church renewal. He suggests that all anyone needs to know can be studied, counted, correlated, and analyzed.

I agree that many hard facts reveal either the health or illness of the church. I have found this kind of material useful in helping churches reach a point of repentance concerning their need for renewal. But the danger of statistical punditry is the belief that the answer lies in the numbers. This information has the same limits as any other kind of data.

For many years it was believed that if a therapist could lead a person into self-discovery, healing was on its way. After gaining insight, the concept taught, each person has the inner resources to overcome his or her problem. In practice the opposite is often the case. Confronted with the inner self, the person often descends into despair and hopelessness. If the ability to heal self lies within a person, then the only resource to believe in is self. This kind of insight proves self-defeating for those who cannot change without outside help.

It's the same in the church. When church consultants help a church reach the conclusion that it is failing, the news can be defeating. Although the numbers reveal the condition of the church and help you compare it to others, this comparison may be fallacious, because those who form the standard may also be doing poorly.

Evangelical mythology is often half or partial truth taught as whole truth. Statistics yield a part of the truth that can be measured. Through their giftedness and life experience, pundits themselves contribute part of truth. But often the statistical pundit is without portfolio when it comes to pastoral experience or understanding the emotional journey of a pastor. Pundits are good at diagnosis but are weak in prognosis. When it comes to prescription, they are hamstrung, because they live out of context to the institution they desire to help. Because a method or idea created explosive growth at one church does not necessarily mean it will create the same forward surge in another. One need heed the words of Mark Twain, "There are three kinds of lies: lies, damn lies, and statistics."

The greatest fear I have about the new priesthood is its redefinition of what is normal. The megachurch pastor says that people don't make commitments anymore, and if we want to be successful, we need to give up on the idea that high commitment is the normal Christian life. The statistical pundit tells us that in the thirty fastest growing churches in our land, the nomenclature of guilt, fear, responsibility, and judgment has been extracted in order to make the secular-minded feel more at home. Because the new priests have such influence, many a needy pastor takes the plunge into such belief systems without running it through his scriptural grid.

Normal then becomes what Christians are experiencing and practicing, not what Scripture teaches *should* be experienced and practiced. No one wants to admit that the normal Christian life has been redefined and downgraded to accommodate culture, but on a practical basis I am afraid that such is the case. In church after church and with pastor after pastor, the belief that the average Christian will be highly committed to the cause of Christ has nearly evaporated.

3

Three Myths about Commitment

Much of contemporary evangelical leadership has either adopted three core myths or at least accepted them as their modus operandi.

Myth 1: People Don't Make Commitments Anymore

There it was, in thirty-six-point type, boldly printed across a photo of a man and woman with perfect bodies. The couple were mounted on treadmills, effortlessly walking their way to health. The powerfully portrayed subliminal message was "Join our health club, and you will look like these marvelous specimens of humankind." What was boldly printed across the ad so as to dominate? NO COMMITMENT!

Only a thoroughly deceived culture like ours would even pretend that such nonsense is true. Of course there is little chance that anyone, regardless of commitment, work ethic, and willingness to sweat, could ever look like the models. While most people would like to be in such good condition, no one but the models themselves really needs it. Even more ridiculous is the notion that such a result could be had without commitment. But some advertiser, who is an expert at creating artificial need, has now created a false promise to entice the unwary. What naive and foolish people is he trying to reach? The demographics of our society say the target is the average American under fifty.

What led a company to spend thousands of dollars to entice the average American with such falsehood? The appalling fact is that Americans have been thoroughly discipled by their culture. The advertising industry has done a masterful job of convincing us that we should have what we cannot have and that we won't need to earn it, deserve it, or wait on it. You need it, you deserve it, and you can have it now. Furthermore, it is your rightful heritage as an American.

Salad-bar Christianity

It is not surprising, then, that Christians have moved in this same shameful direction. Many have sound-bite attention spans. Life is a cafeteria, and the menu is huge.

Church is just another item on the menu, and it competes with a variety of alternatives that often prove much more stimulating, fulfilling, and fun filled. In a culture where even the majority of Christians think that having a good time is more important than missions, leaders are facing a formidable foe. The church competes with warm beaches, snow-capped mountains, scenic lakes, and the comfort of the Serta sleeper. Since the competition for people's time is so fierce, we can't ask for much, or we are in danger of over-challenging them, and they will walk out the door. Sunday school teachers commit for a month, a small group for six weeks, and youth sponsors until it gets difficult. The conventional wisdom is: Don't ask for too much; people are stressed, and they will burn out or drop out.

It's a lie.

People will make serious and extended commitments. Let me say that again. People will make serious and extended commitments. Not only will they make them; they *want* to make them. Everyone is highly committed to one thing or another. In our society, the commitment is usually to self.

As a young pastor I was told that the highly committed were few, and that I should remove the idealistic stars from my eyes. True, many Christians are content to live lives of tedious mediocrity. True, the person "chomping at the bit" to give everything to Christ is rare; I've also experienced the depressive cloud of skepticism that hovered over church leadership. Many frankly told me that my expectations for the church were unrealistic and that after a few educative kicks in the teeth I would agree. In some aspects my jaded counselors were right. But with respect to the fundamental core, they were completely wrong.

My Presupposition

Every Christian wants to obey God, please God, and be fully committed to God. That desire is placed by the residency of the Holy Spirit at spiritual birth (Rom. 8:5–9; 1 Cor. 12:13; Gal. 5:16–18). This desire can be submerged under spiritual inactivity, guilt from disobedience, or extensive sowing to the flesh (Gal. 6:7–9). However, people don't want to spend a life with conflict between their value systems and their practice of life. The fundamental truth that gives hope is that, regardless of how deeply it is buried or damaged, the will to serve and please God is there. I have always believed that if we appeal to that God-given desire, it will be awakened, and Christians will aspire to his service.

This is the crucial linchpin for the leader: Whom do you believe? Do you believe the pundits and demographers who say people won't make commitments, and if you try, they will scatter like the four winds? Or do you trust your theology, which tells you that the fundamental nature of a Christian is to fit into the Savior's plan?

Though I didn't expect every person to be highly committed, I did and do believe that every Christian really desires to be. My experience has shown that where high commitment is taught as normal, as many as 50 to 65 percent will achieve it.

My Experience

Regardless of how many times it is proven false, people insist on telling me, "You can't get people to do that." In my first church, our leaders met once a week at 5:30 A.M., led small groups during the week, and participated in a series of outreaches. The pastorates in which I served were marked by a waiting line to serve and lead. These congregations created an environment that said and supported the idea that leading sacrificially was the highest privilege and calling of the Christian. My conviction was "If you prove yourself, we will let you work harder and longer for Christ."

When I proposed the Vision 2000 Training Network, or T-NET, nearly everyone told me it wouldn't work. I was told, "You will never be able to get churches to make two-year commitments, pay that much money, and seriously engage in the necessary changes to become more effective in their mission." But now, more than 3,000 church leaders have enrolled in T-NET, and 94 percent of the T-NET churches have said the rigor and accountability were worth it all. None of this could have been accomplished without the presupposition, driven by theology, that Christian people desire and will make high commitments. It could not have happened without risk taking based on the belief that God will honor his Word.

Church leaders get what they ask for, prepare for, and truly believe in. If you aim for the heart of a Christian and hit it, his time, his gifts, and his resources will be close behind.

Myth 2: People Have Less Time

Time magazine noted that time could be to the 1990s what money was to the 1980s. An advertisement states, "This is the face of the enemy," next to the picture of a clock. Pollster Lou Harris reported that Americans feel they have less free time than they once did. There are more working women, more single parents, more "latchkey" children, and more parents working separate shifts. . . . There is more to cope with, crowded highways, slower commutes, longer supermarket lines. Time seems to be in short supply; the media speaks of a time famine or of being time-deprived. So stated the *Time* article.

But it's not true.

Data shows that Americans have more free time today than ever. Men have forty hours and women thirty-nine hours per week of discretionary time. Free time is defined as what is left after subtracting time working and commuting to work, taking care of the family, doing housework, shopping, sleeping, eating, and performing other personal-care activities. Free-time activities include the time adults spend going to school or taking part in clubs and other organizations. Watching television, reading, and visiting with friends are choices Americans make with free time. Women are doing less housework; the work week is shorter; and the truth is that *free time is expanding*.[1] *The idea that people have less time for commitment is simply false.* This means that, in general, people have more time to give to the cause of Christ.

Another finding also slaps the myth in the face: The Gallup Poll found that the number-one choice of Americans for volunteer work is the church. That should be good news to every pastor and church leader.

So those who tell us that Christians won't make high commitments anymore are wrong in at least three ways:

1. They are wrong theologically, for people do desire to make their lives count for Christ.
2. They are wrong factually, in that people have more free time than ever.
3. They are wrong about the willingness of the general Christian population to serve in the church.

Theology, the actual time available, and the desire of the general population all are on the side of high and serious commitment. To continue to allow the naysayers to dictate our lives is simply foolish and wrong.

This does not mean, however, that there are no people who are very busy or too busy. It simply comes down to choice. Usually, people who say they are too busy are. Their lives are filled with the busyness they have chosen, and they can choose to be busy for God or busy without God. The Christian populace needs to be lovingly confronted with the facts; preferably, it should be a loving and sensitive confrontation via the Scriptures.

Some obvious differences exist among people. Younger married people with four children are much more stressed and time pressed than the empty nesters in their fifties. Single people have more free time than married couples. A dual-earner couple with children has a more "packed" schedule than does a couple in which only one spouse works. Nevertheless, the church is in need of a bit of reality therapy on the time and commitment issue.

Myth 3: Some People Can Build Commitment in Others, but Not Me!

The first two myths are what the journalists, demographers, pundits, and other members of the priestly pantheon of experts tell us. This third myth is what too many church leaders are telling themselves.

After addressing a group of leaders on this topic, I've been told many times, "Bill, you must have had the natural leaders." "Your church must have been located in an area conducive to growth." "You must have worked in an open culture, where people relished change." "You don't understand; it's tougher where I am." "What works for you won't work for me." If you have that attitude, I agree. If you don't think you can do it, you're right. But if you think you can do it, you're right again.

Another thing I frequently hear is the lament, "If only I had your leaders, if only I had the money, if only I lived where you lived and had the opportunity you had." If only, if only, if only. An "if only" mentality gives birth to an "if only" ministry and results in an "if only" life.

How do Christian leaders allow themselves to fall into this deplorable state of deterioration? There are three reasons why they find themselves in this predicament.

The "Spirit of the Age" Has Dulled Their Vision

Circumstances have chewed the heart out of many pastors' core beliefs. They have simply lost heart that God can use them to make a difference. Because they have failed so often in building commitment in others, they can no longer face the disappointment. Failure has become a form of rejection that hurts so much and so deeply that they will do whatever it takes to get it to stop. Even accommodation to the behavioral level of the semiobedient believer and crafting a diluted theology that doesn't remind them of their shortfalls are acceptable—to end the pain. In short, their experiences have led them to defeat, and because they have seen so little success, they have given up efforts at developing leadership. Few realize that lack of leadership training is where the fault lies, and that is where they need to start.

One of the keys to building commitment is the development of a special environment that nurtures and trains leaders. For it to work, people are required to meet twice a month and engage in related work experiences. This community of leaders must be special. Not everyone who wants in can participate.

The disappointing truth is once you have explained to leaders what it takes to build other leaders, their first inclination is to tell you they can't do it. Even if you give them the map, they may not be willing to make the journey. They have lost their vision, have misplaced their confidence, and have forgotten their theology. To put it into the biblical vernacular they "lose heart." The fourth chapter of Paul's second letter to the Corinthian church begins and ends with this expression. People lose heart because they are beaten around by difficulty and disappointment. Paul's words are quite descriptive: "pressed in on every side," "perplexed," "persecuted," "struck down"; while the opposition is challenging, Paul is not "crushed," "in despair," "abandoned," or "destroyed." Paul and others who follow his prescription are not knocked out of ministry because they have the two strengths that every servant of God should possess:

1. *The realization that ministry is a gift.* We don't own it; we simply serve. What counts is our faithfulness. Everything else is safely in the hands of God (2 Cor. 4:1).
2. *An eternal perspective.* The Christian leader sees beyond the material. Unbelievers are blinded to spiritual truth; what appears to be happening is not what is actually happening. What appears to be a decaying culture dominated by the pursuit of pleasure is really a mass of desperate people in search of meaning. The breakthrough then comes when we recognize this truth and turn negative passion and energy into a positive flow.

Christians are often blinded to what is really significant. Younger evangelicals often want to scale the spiritual heights, but they also want to get there quickly and without too much effort. They want it with all the cultural trappings of success. In other words, they want to be biblical scholars without study, spiritually mature without discipline, and to store up treasure in heaven while pouring all their money into the stock market, the second home, and exotic vacations. The spiritual leader can turn this around in many people. Though it is naive to think that a wholesale change will be experienced in everyone, a great deal of progress can be made. In the long run, whatever difficulty is presently ours is of little consequence (2 Cor. 4:16–18).

Of course the antidote is for each discouraged or possibly jaded spiritual leader to draw two full lungs of fresh and invigorating biblical air, gaining the courage and the heart to try again. A leader's responsibility is to give people a reason to change behavior. Leadership that only offers committee membership or Sunday school socials won't make any difference. Under those circumstances, when church members continue on their narcissistic way, who can blame them?

People Actually Believe Their Excuses

I was a collegiate basketball player. As the years pass, my memories of some of my athletic exploits tend to change—almost always for the better. I seem to have increased my jumping ability, shooting percentage, and competitive edge. Today it is easy to imagine what it was like then. When someone asks, "Could you have played in the pros?" my memory answers, "Of course, but I chose instead to serve the Lord."

This memory lapse (or should I say memory disfigurement) led one church to present me with a custom-made

T-shirt. Across the front it said, "The older I get, the better I was."

It is human nature to embellish the past, rewrite history to our liking, and after a while believe it really happened that way. This same deceptive part of our natures works in other areas as well. Criminals claim innocence and refuse to take personal responsibility for their actions. Psychology finds excuses, and thus there are no criminals, but only victims of society. In fact, we are all victims, and this psychological kick has spawned a nation of victims, rather than responsible adults. When the darker side of human nature joins with the falsehood of our popular culture, you produce a partnership that destroys truth, personality, and the ability to grow responsibly. To build Christian commitment, church leaders must return people to the truth about their lives.

You may have read about the study that asked high school students to rank themselves in math ability, in contrast to other nations. Korean youth rated themselves low on the international scale; American teens rated themselves first. The reality was that Koreans were first and Americans in the bottom third.

This reminds me of the late Jamie Buckingham's pithy statement, "First the truth will make you miserable, then it will set you free." Many are living higher-stress lives, but the high stress results from their perception rather than reality.

First, then, those who are convinced they have less time, more stress, and fewer options need a dose of the truth. This is risky, because they have been lying to themselves for so long they now hold their excuses as bone-deep convictions.

YOU'RE NOT TOO BUSY FOR GOD

True, people feel busy, and many actually are. Stress, however, can make six hours of work seem like twelve.

When laced with stress, many normal activities can drain all physical and emotional strength. Most often, however, the "stressed out" are living undisciplined, unstructured lives. They dabble in the spiritual disciplines and therefore are somewhat spiritually schizophrenic. They have good intentions, but they are not positioned to reach their own goals. True, their free time is gone, but how are they spending that time? Too often they fritter it away on undisciplined activity.

During my time as a leader, several "too busy" people have challenged me. Since I advocate that we all find time to do what is important to us, I sometimes meet with resistance.

When a person says, "I am too busy to make a commitment to spiritual growth or service," my return shot is, "Let's take a look at your schedule." In almost every case I have found that the person has found time for golf, attendance at sporting events, and other fun activities. I believe that people need recreational activity and other ways to relax, but they also spend hours watching television and waste even more time in unproductive activity that could be delegated. When they sit down and actually see how much discretionary time they have, it is embarrassing and shocking, but hopeful.

GOOD INTENTIONS

Repeating the same behavior over and over again, while expecting different results, is insanity. If you bang your head against the wall once and discover that it hurts, you don't need to do it again. But people fall into this trap time and time again. I firmly believe that negative behaviors keep well-intentioned people from deepening their walk with God and from increasing their productivity for God.

Many who practice self-defeating behaviors have no intention of engaging in them again and don't mean to be self-destructive. The alcoholic doesn't intend to destroy himself; he just wants a drink or two. The overeater doesn't plan to gain more weight and go into depression. In a similar way the materialistic Christian who desires to give 10 percent to the work of Christ and his kingdom doesn't intend to create so much debt she cannot give but a meager amount. Most of the above people are full of good intentions. But good intentions are not enough; they don't get the job done. Though they are the beginning of positive change, good intentions must be supported by structured plans to succeed. Christians who wrongly think that their problem is not having enough time to do what they intend to should be introduced to three things: the truth via scrutiny of their schedules, the restructuring of their schedules, and the willing submission to a person or group who will help them keep their new commitments. For true behavioral change and the development of Christlike character, such structure is vital. A life without discipline is a disaster.

The Perfect Moment

When it comes to commitment, two primary deceptions plague the contemporary disciple. The first is the problem of time; the person thinks he or she does not have enough of it. The second is that the person believes that there will someday come the time, the "perfect moment," when he or she will. When that moment comes, like a falling star, an unexpected visitor, or a winning lottery ticket, it just happens. This is one of those silly ideas that humankind grasps and pulls to its breast. It gives hope, though a false hope. Many people live life waiting for their proverbial ship to come in. Unfortunately it seldom does.

This false hope is so insidious because it is amorphous. It takes on the shape of the person's life at any given time. The young are busy building life; they must serve the company to get into a position where they can make better choices. The young family, of course, must give priority to their relationships and the new arrivals. The middle-age family needs even more income, because the kids are getting ready to go to college. Father is probably rising in the corporate world or building his business, and Mother is both teacher and chauffeur, if she's not employed elsewhere. This is followed by the college years. Grandchildren come, and Grandfather and Grandmother are still waiting for that perfect moment. The perfect moment is that moment when nothing important in your life is competing with serving and giving. Before you know it, you're either too sick or too dead. In the end you ask the question, "What happened?" and add, "We certainly intended to do more."

The myth of the perfect moment is destructive to both the individuals who hold it and to the church they attend. Surgery is required by a loving and skilled leader, who with the scalpel of Scripture and the guidance of the Holy Spirit, extracts this deadly myth from the body of Christ.

You Get What You Prepare For

Jesus walked by the Sea of Galilee and called out to Peter and Andrew, "Come, follow me . . . and I will make you fishers of men. At once they left their nets and followed him" (Matt. 4:19).

At my first reading of this passage I was impressed with Jesus' supernatural ability to know in advance that Peter and Andrew would follow him. I still do not doubt that Jesus knew they would follow him, but as I studied the Scripture more, I saw something else. Soon I became equally impressed with how Jesus prepared Peter and Andrew for this crucial moment. Then I discovered something else, and this third imprint on my soul has made the deepest impression on me. In fact, I have found it vital to leadership. That third impression is the principle "You get what you prepare for."

Many people live by the axiom "You get what you ask for," but I find it both untrue and counterproductive.

Living by this creed means you do not get very much. Effective recruitment is a matter of preparation and timing, not a matter of asking. Generally, leaders ask for too much too soon. They often operate on the assumption that somehow God will tap people on the shoulder as soon as they mention an opportunity. The problem is that the majority of people would need a pillar of fire at night and a cloud by day, accompanied by a thunderous voice barking instructions, to prompt them to say yes immediately. Normally this method takes place from the pulpit, in the form of an impassioned plea to missionary service, sacrificial giving, or high, long-term commitment. I believe people will make high and long commitments, but not at the entry level. So by asking people for too much too soon, leaders not only get unsatisfactory results, they reduce the possibility that the overwhelmed will be open to the next appeal. If somehow they have used guilt or accused the unwilling of being unspiritual, great damage will have been done. In such cases, the resurrection of damaged motivation is very difficult.

I remember too vividly the first year I worked with college students. I was privileged to introduce a college freshman to Christ. He was ready; it was like picking ripe fruit. He was excited about what he had done and what it meant. Two days later, he was eager to get together for a follow-up meeting. I found him so on fire, so hot for the things of God that I launched into an inspired sermonette (at least I thought it was inspired) on what God might lead a choice young man like himself to do. In a moment of sheer enthusiasm, I told him that God would want him to be a missionary or engage in pastoral work.

That is the last time I saw him, except for that time on campus when I called his name and he ducked behind a group of students. Since I am tall, he could always see me first. He wouldn't return my calls or attend any meetings. I had blasted this choice young man with too much too soon, and today he may not be serving God, partly because of my stupidity.

The other extreme is to ask for too little too late. This stems from the belief that people probably won't respond, but we suppose we should ask for some commitment anyway. It's a deflated belief system. It is like owning a sailboat but believing the wind doesn't really blow.

The axiom to remember is not "You get what you ask for" but "You get what you prepare for."

Know Your Audience

The other concept that Jesus taught us is to remember whom you are talking to.

The reasons the men dropped their nets to follow Jesus then are the same reasons they drop whatever they have to follow Jesus now:

1. They had already been with Jesus.
2. He called them into a relationship to himself.
3. He recruited them to a vision, not a job.

It is the first of these three reasons that I want to explore in this book.

Jesus knew the men he challenged to drop everything and follow him. These are the men who sought him out when John the Baptist said, "Look, the Lamb of God!" (John 1:35). When the two followed Jesus, he asked them what they wanted. They responded with a silly question, "Where are you staying?" This is like asking for someone's phone number. They really wanted to ask, "Are you the Messiah, the promised one?"

Jesus knew what they wanted, but instead of giving them too much too soon, he simply responded, "Come . . .

and you will see" (John 1:39). For the next four to six months Jesus introduced these new followers to three things:

1. A relationship to himself.
2. The nature of ministry.
3. The challenge of mission.

During this period Jesus answered their questions, and they learned from him.

At the end of the time, Jesus issued what I call the embryonic Great Commission. The followers had just returned from town with food. The woman Jesus had just engaged in conversation at the well probably passed them, eagerly going to town to get others to come and meet a prophet. When the disciples asked if he wanted food, he responded with a remarkable statement: "My food is to do the will of him who sent me and to finish his work. Do you not say, 'Four months more and then the harvest?' I tell you, open your eyes and look at the fields! They are ripe for harvest" (John 4:34–35).

After this declaration of his mission, Jesus sent them home to continue their normal work. But the fish began to stink; those long hours on the sea grew boring; the mending of nets and the other duties of a fisherman started to lose their appeal and meaning. In their more reflective moments, they probably remembered their time with Jesus as the most exciting and purposeful experience of their lives.

So when Jesus approached them to follow him, they were more than ready; they were eager, even anxious to get started. He knew the men he was talking to, and they were primed and ready.

The principle is that you get what you prepare for. They were prepared for higher commitment because they'd experienced meaningful low commitment. When people start with low, short-term commitment, they can be nudged up to longer and higher commitment. *If you want high, long-term commitment, you ask the already committed. You get there by securing short-term low commitment from the uncommitted. The key is knowing who you are talking to and what you want them to do.*

Avoid simply complaining about the deplorable state of people's commitment level. You can get them to be highly committed; in fact, God expects you to do it.

4

The Top Ten Enemies of Building High Commitment

Comedian David Letterman and I played on the same high school basketball team. Dave was not our best player, but he was our funniest player, and now he's our richest one. Would you believe that I gave Dave the idea for his now famous Top Ten List? (I hope you don't, because I didn't. The first time I heard it was on television, just like you.)

However, now that I have your attention, I would like to have you consider the top ten enemies of building high commitment in the church. We'll start with Number 10, just as Dave does. Even though Number 1 should be and will always be our most difficult enemy, these are not listed in order of importance. Some I have mentioned in earlier chapters, but since these enemies need to be grouped together on one list, I am doing it here.

Enemy Number 10: The Dismissal of Theology

We live in a very dangerous time for evangelicals. When the word *theology* is used in a local church, it is usually referred to negatively, or at least people are encouraged to yawn. Those who speak negatively of theology believe that by so doing they can become relevant to the unreached. With the best of intentions, I believe, they are attempting to break out of the institutional parameters that hold the church back from effective outreach. They would say that while theology is needed, very few in the church care about it, and certainly the unchurched have no interest in our theology. Such leaders make a very convincing argument: They are trying to meet the needs of hurting people, and since theology seems irrelevant to these people, it can be ignored.

Of course they couldn't be any more wrong: Theology is both vitally important and crucially relevant in our society today.

If we swallow the line of thinking that denigrates theology, we fall into the same trap liberal ministers fell into when they mistakenly identified their ineffectiveness in reaching people as an irrelevant-message problem. So they changed their message to one of compassion without moral requirements or absolutes dealing with reconciliation to God. Their new stance came to be known as the "social gospel." While a great need for compassion and meeting social needs exists, that is not a person's deepest need. Therefore, liberals found themselves in a subjective world, a needs-on-demand society with no real, objective basis on which to make decisions. They lost their message.

Contemporary evangelicalism is on the same slippery slope. It is in danger of becoming so identified with its culture that it is losing its soul. Evangelicalism is deeply enculturated in at least two ways:

1. It has adopted its own negative subcultural ethos of self-contemplation, self-service, and self-isolation.
2. It is unaware of the deleterious effects of secularism and pluralism.

Secularization brings materialism and the psychologization of the church. Pluralism brings relativism and breaks the back of absolute truth. Without absolute spiritual truth, the church remains in bondage and has no real message of liberation (John 8:31–32).

Thus, sad to say, evangelicals are now in danger of losing their message. If we tailor our message to the perceived needs of the congregation and/or of the world, we are going to find ourselves regularly changing our message in order to accommodate the cultural sense of priority. The sure way to be irrelevant is to be an echo chamber for society. Society tells us what it feels on the spur of a particular moment, and we respond in kind. The only way to be relevant on an ongoing basis is to have an eternal message. The basis of that eternal message, founded on absolute truth, is called theology.

Let Scripture Set the Agenda

We should remember that although the Scriptures are inspired, theology is not. But our understanding of God and the absolutes of Scripture must drive the church. Rather than being a seeker-driven church, a market-driven church, or a need-driven church, we must seek to become a theologically driven church. Let Scripture and nothing else set our agenda. Then within the parameters of Scripture, let us touch and understand the market around us, the needs that confront us, and the society in which we live. Let's remove our theology from our church closets, dust it off, breathe new life into it, and move forward with an eternal, objective, solid agenda.

Regarding the importance of theology, I certainly can't say it any better than C. S. Lewis did several decades ago:

> Everyone has warned me not to tell you what I am going to tell you. . . . They all say, "The ordinary reader does not want Theology; give him plain practical religion." I have

rejected their advice. I do not think the ordinary reader is such a fool. Theology means "the science of God" and I think any man who wants to think about God at all would like to have the clearest and most accurate ideas about him which are available. You are not children: why should you be treated like children?

In a way I quite understand why some people are put off by Theology. I remember once when I had been giving a talk to the R.A.F., an old, hard-bitten officer got up and said, "I've no use for all that stuff. But, mind you, I'm a religious man too. I know there's a God. I've felt him, out alone in the desert at night, the tremendous mystery. And that's just why I don't believe all your neat little dogmas and formulas about him. To anyone who's met the real thing they all seem so petty and pedantic and unreal."

Now in a sense I quite agreed with that man. I think he had probably a real experience of God in the desert. And when he turned from that experience to the Christian creeds, I think he really was turning from something real to something less real. In the same way, if a man has once looked at the Atlantic from the beach, and then goes and looks at a map of the Atlantic, he also will be turning from real waves to a bit of colored paper. But here comes the point. The map is admittedly only colored paper, but there are two things you have to remember about it. In the first place, it is based on what hundreds and thousands of people have found out by sailing the real Atlantic. In that way it has behind it masses of experience just as real as the one you could have from the beach; only while yours would be a single isolated glimpse, the map fits all those different experiences together. In the second place if you want to go anywhere, the map is absolutely necessary. As long as you are content with walks on the beach, your own glimpses are far more fun than looking at the map. But the map is going to be of more worth than walks on the beach if you want to get to America.

Now Theology is like the map. Merely learning and thinking about the Christian Doctrines, if you stop there, is less real and less exciting than the sort of thing my friend got in the desert. Doctrines are not God; they are only a kind of map. But the map is based on the experience of hundreds of people who really were in touch with God—experiences compared with which any thrills or pious feelings you or I are likely to get on our own way are very elementary and very confused. And secondly, if you want to get any further you must use the map. You see, what happened to that man in the desert may have been real and was certainly exciting but nothing comes of it. It leads nowhere. There is nothing to do about it. In fact, that is just why a vague religion—all about feeling God in nature and so on—is so attractive. It is all thrills and no work, like watching the waves from the beach. But you will not get to Newfoundland by studying the Atlantic that way, and you will not get eternal life by simply feeling the presence of God in flowers or music. Neither will you get anywhere by looking at maps without going to sea. Nor will you be very safe if you go to sea without a map.[1]

Enemy Number 9: Existing Pastoral Training

Two pathologies presently being perpetuated in pastoral training have led to serious weakness in our evangelical churches. They are the pulpit-driven church and the pulpit-dependent church.

The Pulpit-Driven Church

In a pulpit-driven church, the church's numerical growth is dependent on the pastor's preaching ability. The results are thousands of churches that are 100 to 150 members in size. Nothing is wrong with a church of this size, if it has reached its full potential in its community. The fact is that most churches limit themselves quite severely in this regard.

In seminary I was taught that if we preached sermons like our more luminous graduates we would have growing churches. This was and still is true among the more talented, those on whom God has bestowed great communicative gifts. But for the majority of mere mortals who faithfully preach well-prepared sermons each week, it is not true. To think of the pulpit as the primary growth tool of the church can lead to unfair expectations on the pastor and ultimately to his receiving both the blame and the frustration for a declining or stalled-out church.

God calls his people to gather in church for training and to strengthen the living community. They then are enabled to work in ministry. They find their true purpose in going into the harvest field, not just as residents but as workers. They find themselves reaching out to people, and those people come to know Christ and are brought to the church. New Christians are not there primarily because of the pastor's preaching ability, even though the pastor's sermons reach them, touch them, and minister to them. Developing such a church is not a matter of eloquence but of pastoral effectiveness in training and developing people.

We need to abolish the concept that churches grow primarily through preaching and focus on church growth through the church populace doing evangelism where they live, work, and play.

The Pulpit-Dependent Church

In the second pathology, the pulpit-dependent church, the membership depends on the pastor's sermons for its spiritual food. A pastor's sermons should be well-crafted and relevant, rooted in Scripture, and applied in the trenches of life. But when church members say, "The pastor isn't feeding me, and that is the reason I am unhappy, not growing spiritually, and generally losing my focus as a believer," this is usually a fleshly canard. It is usually a form of projection of responsibility on to another and a pathetic attempt at self-exoneration. Such an attitude has led to a generation of pulpit-dependent Christians who have substituted the Sunday sermon for a personal devotional life. Therefore, they have an "arm's length" relationship with Christ, which is evidenced in both spiritual anemia and a preoccupation with the faults and foibles of their spiritual leaders.

After being taught to study the Bible on their own, Christians should find their daily spiritual diet in regularly reading, studying, memorizing, and meditating on God's Word. Then the sermon becomes the extra vitamin boost that makes the believer's diet more nutritious. It instructs in the areas of related biblical subjects that are generally out of the reach of the average person's education. The sermon becomes the motivational time in which the tribal leader of the congregation connects with his people. That's exciting, that's good. But let's release ourselves from the bondage of depending on the Sunday sermon for our primary spiritual diet.

It is time for us to change, to move from these pathologies to scriptural principles. Instead of depending on the pastor's preaching to grow the church, we need to adopt the scriptural principle of the people evangelizing their communities and then bringing their converts to church. Instead of pulpit-dependent churches, where individuals substitute the sermon for their devotional life, we need to adopt the spiritual principle of people feeding themselves with the daily intake of God's Word.

Enemy Number 8: The Megachurch Model

There is a great deal to learn from successful leaders. They often break new and important ground in developing and reaching people. That is why thousands of church leaders who are hungry for more effective ministries flock to the megachurch for methods, programs, and inspiration, always hoping that some of that good stuff will "rub off." There may be some wisdom in asking the chairman of General Motors how to run your Kool-Aid stand, but it is also possible that his advice would be worthless. Great differences between contexts make transferability a serious challenge. Therefore, there is very little danger and much to be gained if the example and counsel of the megachurch are first passed through the following filter.

Context and Chemistry

By *context*, I mean the circumstances of the church, such as socioeconomic strata, rural or city, urban or suburban setting, the age of the church, tradition, spiritual condition of the church, or general condition of the church facility and its potential for expansion. By *chemistry*, I mean the unity of the congregation, but even more the relationships of the leadership. Does the pastor relate well with the leaders? Are the appointed leaders and staff properly placed to work in their areas of giftedness? Are they assigned the appropriate work? Sometimes church leaders confront me, saying: "Bill, it didn't work for me. I tried your stuff. My board resisted, and my congregation didn't respond." Every one of the disappointed leaders made the same mistake: They took my working model and attempted to impose it on their system. Working models almost always fail when they are plopped down in different contexts.

The success of a megachurch pastor must be understood in its context. The majority of working models that invite emulation are church plants. That is wonderful; the problem, however, is that most pastors are not church planters and have to deal with very complex, rigid structures. That is why the most important principles to be learned are those that can be reproduced and utilized in any context.

Personality and Gifts

The distressing truth about contemporary pastoral role models is that in large part they cannot be reproduced. The men who are presented at conferences as worth listening to are largely charismatic, highly gifted servants. They are uniquely gifted in their natural talents. Their personalities and gifts cannot be folded up in wrapping paper, placed in a box, and sent home for the price of registration. Through discussions with various leaders of international status, I have had this confirmed multiple times. Some of them hold conferences for pastors because they want to help and because their advice is in demand. Almost to a person they share the same frustration of very different pastors from very different churches, who try to cram the megachurch success model down the throat of a church that has its mouth closed.

The great danger is impersonation instead of imitation. We are familiar with the embarrassment we feel for an Elvis impersonator. The ecclesiastical equivalent is the less well-equipped pastor who impersonates a successful pastor or tries to duplicate his high-tech entertainment with only average resources.

Spirituality and Character

An often-overlooked factor in church growth is the spiritual character of the creative personality. It is superficial to consider the highly gifted as only "flash and dash." The personal life of the creative/entrepreneur pastor will eventually reveal itself. Popularity will erode human veneer. The pressures that come with success will drive the true nature of a person to the surface. That may take years, as culture slowly eats away at leaders' biblically based perspective, and they leave behind essentials for the esoteric. The tragic fall of many evangelical leaders can be attributed to their leaving behind their fundamental doctrinal convictions and the simple devotion that brought them success in the first place. Nevertheless, many gifted pastors and leaders have remained faithful; we must never confuse giftedness or creativity with deviance.

The danger for church leaders looking to benefit from

working models is that they can so easily neglect the importance of spiritual character in the process. Godliness and growth come through our own personal life's tapestry of suffering, joy, sorrow, perseverance, tragedy, transformation, and pain. Each of us is being shaped into Christ's image through completely different circumstances, and there is no "working model" for sanctification other than Christ himself. We cannot imitate or impersonate what God is doing in someone else's life. Just as we cannot send the pastor home with a neatly wrapped box of charisma and gifts, so we cannot, with price of registration, send the pastor home with a box of Christian character.

What Is Reproducible?

Paul encouraged the immature Corinthians, "Follow my example, as I follow the example of Christ" (1 Cor. 11:1), and earlier in that epistle he used Timothy as an example of what he meant by imitation. "He will remind you of my way of life in Christ Jesus, which agrees with what I teach everywhere in every church" (1 Cor. 4:17). Paul passed on a set of principles that were to be taught in every church; it was not the passing of personality or personal rights but an example of sound teaching and godliness.

I wonder how many pastors would turn out for a church-growth seminar on sound teaching and godliness? Imitating or impersonating other people, for other reasons, seems to be a greater attraction.

Paul went to great pains in trying to explain to the Corinthians why his simple gospel of Christ and him crucified was not inferior to the charisma and rhetorical skill of the "super apostles" as he called them. Likewise, Timothy's instructions from Paul are not terribly striking or clever. The apostle merely commanded: "The things you have heard me say in the presence of many witnesses entrust to reliable men who will also be qualified to teach others" (2 Tim. 2:2). If we are going to teach church leaders responsibly, it must be with a theology and philosophy of ministry, first, and methods and working models, second. Our set of principles for leadership and outreach, people development and evangelism must follow those espoused by Paul for the corporate church in Ephesians 4:11–16.

THE STRIPPED-DOWN MODEL

The megachurch is like a Cadillac that has all the "whistles and bells," completely outfitted with every extra that money can buy. But the crucial question is not what paint job it has or how impressive the automobile appears; the crucial question is, What makes the car run effectively? The megachurch should not set the agenda for the church. The Scriptures should do that. Strip away the example of context and leadership chemistry, the personality and giftedness of the leaders; remove the nontransferable spiritual character of the primary leader; and whatever you have left are the basics that make the church go. Take the basic, transferable scriptural principles and outfit your church with the extras that fit who you are as a leader and that suit your context.

We should be thankful for God's blessing on certain ministries, which distinguishes them from others. But God doesn't clone ministries. To think that he does is insulting to him and does violence to his creative work in us. Because the megachurch has a tremendous gravitational pull, it threatens to pull many hungry pastors into the trap of cultural relevancy as the highest good. Let Scripture set the agenda, and then take what works for you from those experiencing various kinds of success. This will protect you from bondage to methods and from success that is rooted in cultural compromise.

Enemy Number 7: The Market-Driven Church

Relevance is the most important thing in market-driven churches. For them to live is to be relevant. They are so driven to succeed that the end justifies the means. Since the ultimate goal is to reach the unreached, it doesn't matter what they have to compromise in order to attain it, even if it leads to some theologically questionable accommodations.

What drives the church both dictates and predicts its future. If the market drives the church, then culture is in control. The mood of our contemporary culture, particularly dominated by media, will define relevance and meaning.

In a secular culture such as ours, why would anyone want the market to drive the church? This philosophy sounds like the worn-out, useless, and finally discarded motto of the World Council of Churches: "The world sets the agenda for the church." With their churches in an attendance free fall, they were smart enough to throw such nonsense overboard. Now evangelicals have picked up the banner of cultural relevance and, like a bunch of fools, are about to repeat the liberals' folly. The very folly we scorned, preached against, and wondered how anyone could so stupidly accept—this is the folly we are adopting.

The liberals' folly was to change theology, the evangelicals' folly is to ignore it. Evangelicals will not change theology; that's what makes us evangelical. Rather, we use it as a security blanket as we launch out onto the ever-changing sea of culture, seeking the new world of relevance. This is manifested in several ways.

Let me explain one. It is very much in vogue for a consultant to ask church leaders, "What do you want your church to be? Figure out your needs and desires, tell me where you want to go, and I will help you craft a philosophy that will take you there." Such people are asking the wrong question! The right question is, In Scripture, what does God say the church is? Based on that, we need to ask, Where should it go and how should it behave? Then we must ask, What does Scripture define as a need and how should it be met?

I believe most evangelicals would have no argument with looking first to Scripture. But we cannot safely assume that this task is ever seriously undertaken. Most churches venture no further than their prepackaged and often predigested denominational doctrinal statement. The crafting of a philosophy of ministry based on Scripture is very rare. Doing that kind of theology takes time, effort, and a serious commitment.

Those evangelicals who first employed and popularized the term "market driven" did so with good intentions. The idea is to understand your market so more people can be reached for Christ. I also know that the progenitors of this concept have a strong evangelical theology. The problem, however, is what impression "market driven" leaves and what it leaves out, namely theology. A market-sensitive, theologically driven church is much preferred. As usual, the problem occurs at the "user level." The commonly accepted definition is not what the originators meant by "market-driven church," but it's what thousands are doing under that label. Let's put first things first: Start with theology and then seek to understand the market.

When the Audience Is Sovereign

If the market provides your direction, your listeners write your sermons. What do people want to hear? What should we not say? Most surveys tell us that the general public does not like church because it is boring and because they don't see its relevance to their lives. The general public, according to these surveys, feel that the church makes them feel guilty, and it is always asking for money.

So we strive not to offend. First, we must remove inflammatory words from our messages: sin, hell, wickedness, adultery, fornication, judgment. These words are judgmental, smack of absolute truth, and make people feel guilty. Above all, we are told that we must not confront people with their financial responsibility before God.

Too many pastors are far too worried about offending their listeners. Remember that the gospel is offensive to the secular-minded person, and it is impossible to be faithful and avoid offense (2 Cor. 2:16). Paul tells us both that the message stinks in the nostrils of the perishing and that we should be wise and winsome with "outsiders" (Col. 4:5–6). And regardless of the response, we should not be shamed or intimidated by the hearer (Rom. 1:16). What we can avoid are unnecessary offensive words and attitudes. There is a difference between being judgmental and preaching about the reality of judgment.

The danger lies not in our being sensitive to contemporary hearers, nor in our designing interesting sermons that are both relevant and winsome. And it does not show up when we have a clear focus on reaching the unreached. Rather, the danger appears when these things dictate our philosophy and drive our ministry. Paul taught us that in order to reach different people we would need to identify with them (1 Cor. 9:22). On Mars Hill, he modeled a sermon rooted in contemporary Athenian culture (Acts 17). But note that Paul didn't back off his message. Some of the hearers believed, but the majority laughed, sneered, and rejected his proposition of absolute truth. I do not advocate ignoring market trends or the sensitivities of the hearer; neither do I advocate ignoring our theological moorings that give both stability to our message and direction to our ministries. The key to consistent relevance is a commitment to the eternal truths of God's Word.

Demographically Correct

In our effort to "seek and save" our aimless and lost society, evangelicals have sought to use various tools. Demographic study is not new to the world of advertising, but it is now considered "state of the art" among cutting-edge church planters. This is another example of morally neutral tools of technology that can be used by church leaders to better understand their mission field. But when demographics dominates, evangelicals are in danger of valuing demographic correctness over biblical correctness.

Our culture languishes in an environment of political correctness, which leads to a very flat, colorless society. Athletic teams must change their names; language and schoolbooks must be degenderized, free speech sanitized, and all achievement equalized. In its quest to be relevant, the church can become equally boring. In an effort to be all things to all people, we can dilute our message and lose our edge. Christian truth separates, offends, stings, and liberates.

The Drive-in Church

The drive-in church speaks of efforts to create a church without commitment or community. In it people can relate to Christ at arm's length, without entering into the community of Christ or service in that community. Attempts at a literal "drive-in" church are legitimate efforts to do outreach. I have no serious argument with a church that sees it as evangelism, but I would have an argument if it is viewed as an acceptable norm for the Christian life. Christian faith without commitment to the church is inferior Christianity. It is not normal for a Christian to live outside accountability to others and service in the church (Matt. 28:20; Eph. 5:21; 1 Thess. 5:14; 1 Peter 4:10–11).

There is a tendency to accept a new technocratic/psychologized discipleship that says "modern man will only do certain things, given his culture" (technocratic) and "will only respond to getting his needs met" (psychologized). This pollution of the evangelical mind has created large, superficial churches that do little more than cater to the flesh. It does not have to be this way, and thankfully it is not this way in several good megachurches that are driven by a scriptural agenda.

Healthy Christianity is based on truth and is lived out by committed Christians in the context of a local church community. Doing it right costs a lot more in time, money, and grief and is much more challenging. But you do get what you pay for, and the results are much greater when disciples discipline themselves to live and work together for the expansion of the kingdom.

Enemy Number 6: Monolithic Small-Group Theory

Two forces have converged to create the monolithic or every-group-is-the-same mentality. Ironically, those who consider themselves "in touch" with the needs of society and advocate giving people more choices for spiritual development find themselves champions of one kind of group. Not only is it monolithic, but it also violates basic spiritual laws that govern spiritual development. The two forces that have made the monolithic small group popular are:

1. The metachurch movement, or the cell-based church, and its spectacular growth in Korea, Singapore, South Africa, and in some limited way in the United States. The primary reason this method is in vogue is rapid growth. Admittedly, it does provide a way to gather more people faster. There is a place for low-commitment, open small groups, but they should not dominate the small-group life of a church. They are entry level in nature and very limited in developing people.
2. The second force is the speed and superficiality of culture. There is a general belief that people have less time and cannot and will not make long-term, high commitments. Both myths have been addressed and dismissed in earlier chapters. They are repeated here to set the context and make the point. What is wrong with small groups that are open, low in commitment

and short in duration? *Nothing,* if they are part of a larger small-group system that possesses balance.

Miniature Is Mediocre

Anyone can play miniature golf. When someone suggests, "Let's go to the Family Fun Center and play some miniature golf," no one says, "Oh, I haven't played in a long time; I took lessons, but I am a bit rusty." No one speaks of handicaps or throwing clubs or the difficulty of the game. Miniature golf is for everyone and is meant to be fun. After it's over, people laugh and talk about the good time they had. You don't even need golf shoes. In the 1960s I remember a miniature golf tour that was on TV for a while. It didn't last long. People didn't marvel at a great shot; instead, they laughed out loud, slapped their knees, and wondered, *Why would anyone take such an easy game so seriously? Did you see that? How did he get that ball to go through Donald Duck's bill and to exit through Mr. Ed's tail?* Miniature golf didn't make it on TV. It was a novelty, nothing more.

If miniature is normal, then mediocrity becomes normal. When success can be gotten without discipline, it becomes engraved on the hearts of the people that Christianity calls for only mediocre commitment. If people think that commitment is do Bible study if you have time and attend the group if there are no conflicts; if they think that spirituality is getting my needs met, and the highest group value is a feeling of warmth and belonging, then that philosophy will lead to miniature Christians with a miniature mentality. We want Christians to aspire to spiritual greatness. If we want them to play real golf, then we must not encourage them to be satisfied with miniature golf.

Recently I began playing golf in a serious fashion. Throughout my life I have hacked around courses. I watched others and have done my very best every time I have played. Now, however, I am determined to do it right.

I started with a series of lessons, and now I continue to take at least one lesson a month. Every day that I can, I work on the fundamentals and hit golf balls. Whether or not I feel like it, I repeat the same drills in order to develop good habits. This is the only way that I can become a good golfer.

Church leaders must point Christians to the real thing, not miniature versions or cheap substitutes. Christlikeness and spiritual maturity come only with the disciplined practice of holy habits that lead to spiritual greatness. There is no way that responsible leaders can justify low-commitment, short-term, all-open groups as an effective environment for building spiritual disciplines and the creation of Christlikeness. Normal is not what demographers, pundits, and pollsters say is normal. Normal is what Scripture says it is.

Many advocates of the open-groups model of church growth tell us that many aspire to spiritual greatness after being exposed to the open-groups model. It does not surprise me that many do. What *would* surprise me is that many would bolt past the limited challenge of their group and charge into the unknown, without accountability and structure. The majority simply will not go beyond the accepted ethos. Furthermore, they will not go beyond the structures that are provided. In order to mature, they need progressively more challenge.

Advocates will point to the high accountability and challenge they give to their leaders. Admittedly, this system does do a good job of training leaders. But it does a poor job of training the populace. Since about 10 percent of any church are leaders and the remainder followers, a highly trained leadership and a poorly trained, underchallenged populace is unacceptable. Not only does it ignore the call of every Christian to maturity, ministry, and greatness, it is clearly pre-Reformation. Prior to the Reformation, Bibles were not available to the average Christian; they were kept under lock and key in church buildings. As a result, the average believer was kept from interacting with the Scriptures and certainly from the practice of his priesthood. The difference between then and now is that the average Christian has access to Scripture, but the low-demand message of the church community still shuts him or her off from full potential.

A Quicker Harvest

All this is done under the guise of a great harvest. "Look at the people we are reaching. Can't you see the good we are doing?" There is good in a quicker harvest, but since it has no roots, the product is defective. Christians harvested in this manner will not reproduce, and multiplication is lost.

This method, I believe, breaks faith with spiritual laws of sowing and reaping. The Epistle to the Galatians teaches that a person reaps what he sows. We can reap a rich and good harvest or a plethora of negatives. The exhortation is "Let us not become weary in doing good, for at the proper time we will reap a harvest if we do not give up" (Gal. 6:9).

Farmers must follow the laws of sowing and reaping. They cannot "cram" like a student, get lucky and strike it rich in the lottery, go on a crash program for weight loss to get into the swimsuit, or increase workouts to prepare for the first game. They must cultivate the ground, till it, and sow the seed. Then they water, spray, protect, and wait and pray. In its proper time there will be a harvest.

Much of contemporary spirituality is trying to have a microwave harvest. The proponents advocate the "greenhouse" approach. Like agrarian scientists, they use the latest tools, technology, and techniques to create a quicker and larger harvest. But in the end nothing can be successful and sustained unless it submits to the basic physical laws of the farm.

Why then is the monolithic small-group theory the enemy of disciple making? Because it makes acceptable what is scripturally totally unacceptable—mediocre spirituality.

Enemy Number 5: Traditional Church Structure

When structure stops renewal, the structure itself becomes the enemy of the church. Jesus pointed this out to us in Matthew 15:3, when he criticized the Pharisees for holding their traditions higher than the commands of God. Structure can be our best friend or our gravest enemy. The right structure can give wings to the energy that God's Spirit provides for his renewed church. The wrong structure can diffuse that same energy. Many have studied the origins of revival and how to get it started. Though I am motivated to learn about what starts revivals, I am equally interested in what ends them. Much spiritual energy is lost when highly motivated Christians get tired of hitting their heads against church structures that block needed change.

Form Drives Function

In most institutions form drives function. This is normal. That is why organizations struggle with change. The form or method is erroneously identified as the reason for success. This led Peter Drucker to conclude, "The very methods which once created your success eventually destroy your success."

People fondly remember the days when the church parking lot was full on Sunday evenings. They often argue that by maintaining a Sunday-evening service people will again come and bring their unchurched friends. This may be true for a special occasion with a contemporary evangelistic purpose, but it is a losing battle if we think the Christian community is going to return to Sunday-night church service.

George Gallup reports that 45 percent of Protestants and 51 percent of Catholics attend services weekly. But

Gallup apparently neglected to take into consideration the "fudge factor." According to the *American Sociological Review,* many people stretch the truth when answering pollsters about their church attendance.[2] Studies in actual head counts in selected churches found that only 20 percent of Protestants and 28 percent of Catholics are in church each week. Another study measured four religious areas besides church attendance that reveal varying levels of commitment: 19 percent of Americans are religiously committed (practicing their religion regularly), 22 percent are modestly religious, and 29 percent are barely or nominally religious.[3]

We all like to cast ourselves in a slightly better light than is precisely true. When asked about our weight, television-watching habits, or devotional life, precision bows to promotion. Therefore, when you take a congregational poll and 80 percent think a Sunday-night service is good and 50 percent promise to attend, don't get too excited. There is a huge gulf between opinion and desire and an even greater distance between desire and commitment.

Forms that still work don't need to be changed. I don't advocate change for the sake of breaking a spirit of boredom. But for ministry forms that are not producing, change is imperative. In fact, I believe that unwillingness to change to improve ministry is a sin. I know there are early, mid, and late adapters, so I am not saying it is a sin to resist the first time you hear an idea. But stubbornly standing in the way is wrong. The only exception to this would be if the change represented a violation of a clear biblical directive.

Lyle Schaller, Bob Gilliam, and others have recommended that before change is attempted, the situation must be unfrozen. The unfreezing process begins with clarification and review of the church's values. For instance, when people agree they need and desire to reach others for Jesus Christ, you then have a clear, agreed-upon value.

The second step is to show the difference between your values and your performance. Suppose that your highest value is to reach people for Christ, yet there have been only three conversions in the last three years. Maybe your budget is $200,000, and you have 100 people on boards and committees and in teaching assignments. You have employed two pastoral staff and still have just three conversions. In the face of such powerful reality, people start to entertain change.

If you cannot make your case for change, you should not even suggest it. Choose your battles carefully; every change is risky, because it threatens the congregational balance of power. Careful world leaders speak often of geopolitical balance. They make decisions in context, not in isolation. They ask, "How will this decision affect other nations and their relationship to us? Will this action create a higher or lower possibility of war?" They then prudently ask, "Is this worth fighting for and dying for? What is the price tag?"

The third step is to initiate the change. There are many good books and articles on how to best orchestrate the needed change. The phasing in and out of methods should be done with some sensitivity and over a reasonable time period. Many people resist simply because they lack time to process an idea. Proposals often fail because creative early adapters assume everyone processes ideas at their speed and thinks in the same categories they do.

The fourth and last step is to refreeze the situation. This means to institutionalize the change in some meaningful way. Some churches write it into their bylaws. This may be going too far, because it may create a difficulty for future leadership. A more reasonable approach is to publish an annual philosophy of ministry document that goes to all members. This gives changes the needed "clout," yet makes it possible to adjust them at a later date without needless meetings and wrangling.

Function Must Drive Form

I think many Christian leaders try to focus first on scriptural function and then discover the proper forms in the context of their ministry. They often discover that this is not easy to do, because most people are programmatic in their thinking. To be programmatic is not bad; it is not a sign of spiritual weakness; it is simply a matter of "spiritual wiring."

This is why it is important that your leadership be balanced properly. A leadership team composed only of creators and creative developers will blow trumpets and lead thousands into glorious success just before they dive headlong off the cliff into the abyss. There may be immediate success, but disaster is breathing down its neck. If the programmatic alone were in charge, they would simply look for models to copy, and failure would be just as sure to follow. So a balance of the creative conceptualizer and the plodding programmer is the best of all environments. The two will drive each other crazy, but they desperately need each other.

Fall in love with function first; then you can discover the proper forms. If function drives form, then church tradition can never become the enemy; it can be our friend.

Enemy Number 4: User-Friendly Commitment

The term *user-friendly* came into vogue in reference to a visitor's (or seeker's) first experience with the local church. However, what is a good idea for the seeker may be a lousy one for the found.

Most good ideas are easily corrupted. The corruption erupts not with originators, but ironically at the user level. If we become fixated with the seeker, we may thoughtlessly pass on the new laissez-faire attitude to the stagnated saint. If we focus on how easy it is to become part of the church and how easy it is to become a Christian, we need to make sure that we are not changing the requirements of Christian maturity and service, simply to add members to the rolls. Try to remember that once a person enters the Door and begins his spiritual journey, he may progress along various roads. The seeker; the stagnated saint; the broken Christian; the eager learner; the mature, fruitful believer; and the dynamic leader have the same destination but are on different roads. The seeker is determining if he wants to go; the stagnated saint has stopped and stayed at a roadside resort; the eager learner is driving as fast as he can; the mature, fruitful believer is proceeding at peace and with all deliberate speed; the dynamic leader is trying to discern where everyone is and exhorting all to continue. For many, the road is hard and challenging; it requires their best efforts and they find the journey anything but user-friendly.

High commitment is not user-friendly! By definition, *user-friendly* means that learning a skill or reaching a goal is easy the first time and every time. Nothing worthy of honor works that way. You can't cram ten years of experience into a seminar. The notion that a person can mature by taking the fast track is as absurd as trying to eat a year's worth of food in thirty days. The user-friendly approach says that becoming spiritual is like a salad bar. You walk by and take what looks good to you. Being spiritual then becomes what you think is getting your needs met.

Such a microwave mentality destroys discipleship. Many desire Christlikeness, but they want it now and on terms that fit their schedule. If you want a ministry that sounds like one of those cheap electronic organs you can play without knowing how to read music or understand the keyboard—music (of a sort) made quick and easy— you can have it. If you are only looking to hit the right button that will do it all for you, you'll get what you paid for.

On the other hand, commitment costs us everything we have:

Large crowds were traveling with Jesus, and turning to them he said: "If anyone comes to me and does not hate his father and mother, his wife and children, his brothers and sisters—yes even his own life—he cannot be my disciple. And anyone who does not carry his cross and follow me cannot be my disciple."

Luke 14:25–27

Enemy Number 3: Truncated Forms of Disciple Making

Disciple making as a concept has been severely limited in the minds of many (if not most) evangelical Christians, pastors, and leaders. Often a pastor will say, "I'm very interested in discipleship, but I don't know much about it." Another common statement is "We have a discipleship pastor (or program), and I am very supportive." Another revealing phrase is "I am a strong believer in evangelism and discipleship." These statements tell me that the speakers possess less than a robust biblical concept of disciple making. Either by tradition, nomenclature, or neglect they have reduced the Great Commission to a department of their church. It finds its place along with other programs for children and adults. Instead of it being *the* program for the church, it is *a* program in the church.

There is an insidious side to the erosion of biblical nomenclature. It seems harmless to consign the disciple-making concept to a network of small groups or a Sunday school class. What many people mean when they use the term *discipleship* is "a training program for Christians in the basic skills of the Christian faith." Making disciples is, however, the heart of everything the church does. If disciple making can be reduced to another good church activity, then to the degree that we downgrade its preeminence, the enemy wins.

What is most important in your church? Is it preaching? Youth ministry? Helping the sick? Counseling the family?

rting the grief stricken? Support groups? Training
s? Evangelistic outreaches? Through your subjective
you may see two or three as more important, but if
ike ten people from your congregation, you will probably find a wide diversity of views. The trap is to allow
disciple making to be put on the activity list rather than
the purpose list. Making disciples does not belong on the
list, because every activity listed is part of a larger mission
to make disciples.

Disciple making, then, is the heart of the church and it
provides the intentional target toward which the leadership can aim. Whenever we make small what God meant
to be big, we do ourselves and his kingdom a disservice.
Disciple making is not one of the things a church does; it
is what the church does. It is his plan for building a healthy
church and his strategy for evangelizing the world.

Enemy Number 2: Secularization

Secularization is the process by which religion's influence on culture is reduced. Its effect is to bring culture to
a point of indifference to religion and to render religion
irrelevant to public policy as it touches schools and local,
state, and national government. The process is a slow trans-
fer from an ecclesiastical to a civic culture. The United
States Constitution's first amendment guarantees freedom
of religion. However, because of secularization, indifference has become hostility, and freedom of religion has
become freedom from religion.

The most deleterious effect of secularization is how it
changes the attitudes of church members. Mobility, for
instance, has had both a positive and negative result on
spiritual life. The same mobility that allows Billy Graham
to speak to millions also permits Christians to travel on
weekends and neglect the work of their local churches. The
same technology that beams positive Christian teaching

into thousands of homes also keeps many at home who should be in attendance at their local church.

There are three paramount clashes between the effects of culture on the church and disciple making.

The Elevation of Choice to the Highest Virtue

I have written on this at length in chapter 1. What bears repeating is my concern that an act of the will has been elevated to a status above standard virtues. Choice has been given a place above self-discipline, self-denial, honesty, and faithfulness; in fact, choice has even superseded the biblical commandment not to shed innocent blood. While evangelicals don't go as far as their nonbelieving friends, we have made some adjustments to our thinking. This has led to the abandonment of the standard expectations that everyone should practice the same set of spiritual habits such as Bible reading, prayer, stewardship, service, accountability, etc. Therefore, spirituality becomes self-directed, and being spiritual becomes whatever each individual chooses to make it. This leads to superficial Christianity. The only road to spiritual depth and maturity is a road of consistency and self-discipline.

Individualism and a Loss of Interdependence

Secularization has dealt a devastating blow to the Christian community. Mobility of society has led most of us to a larger, more superficial circle of friends. I now have hundreds of friends that I barely know, instead of a few friends with whom I live honestly and deeply, in true accountability. Along with mobility has come its glitzy, relative materialism.

All of us live in a material world and we acknowledge that God has created this world. Therefore, in and of itself, it is a moral good. But whenever we make a cause or pursue something too much, it becomes an "ism," and it takes on a life of its own.

Materialism is part of Western culture, and all who live in this culture—including Christians—are affected. Christians tend to take on cultural mores but in a less extreme form. Secular advertisers, filmmakers, and fashion designers point us toward certain "lifestyles." They've created our wants to such an extent that our wants become our needs. We "need" a bigger and better living space. Today people spend millions of dollars on products they had no idea they needed five years ago. It would never have occurred to us that we needed 50 percent of what we have, if television, magazine, newspaper, and direct-mail advertising hadn't informed us. As a result, many Christians are not able to say yes to God's calling to service because they must work to pay the bills for products they really don't need.

This self-imposed imprisonment has locked away a good share of the Christian labor force in the prison of materialism. Instead of God getting their best, mammon gets their premium time and thinking. Time for God and time to build helpful, supportive relationships is lost.

Instant Gratification

We live in a drive-up, drive-through world. Everything from Jiffy Johns to Jiffy Lube communicates speed and service. But one thing can't be done in a jiffy: spiritual maturity. There is a natural order and rate of speed to maturity.

According to Robert Clinton, convergence is the process by which life experience, our place in the life cycle, and our spiritual training and ministry portfolio come together to that "for this I was born" experience. This is a normal process, if we make steady progress throughout our twenties and thirties. Sometime in our early forties convergence takes place, and what should follow are twenty plus years of fruitfulness and satisfaction.

However, our culture militates against this process. Part of the culture war is the struggle of Christians to live at a different rate of speed with respect to important results.

The enculturation of Christians is revealed in their desire to want the church to be faster, have more sparkle, give more emotional pleasure, and to self-indulge felt need. Leaders often feel tempted to accept and accommodate church programming that addresses immediate felt need, instead of that which meets long-term real need. The insidious nature of instant maturity is that it can be excused under the guise of reaching others for Christ. The effect this has on the church is put so well by George MacDonald: "That need which is no need is a demon sucking at the spring of your life." The need for spiritual speed in maturation is no need at all.

It is imperative for Christian leaders to understand the maturity process by reaching convergence themselves. Then they must create a church ethos that encourages true growth, which in turn will lead to a consistent labor force that can reap a great spiritual harvest.

We must stand against the negative dividends secularization provides. Against choice as the highest virtue we are to bring immutable standards that demand us to choose right or wrong. Against the deleterious effects of individualism we must build community, sharing life with others in a loving and supportive way. Against instant gratification we must offer delayed but better results. We are building a house on the rock rather than on changing cultural sand, even though building sand castles is easier and quicker. Although we don't aspire to a religious culture, we do desire to be a spiritual people who positively affect our culture.

Enemy Number 1: The World, the Flesh, and the Devil

The obvious truth is that the greatest enemy is the unholy trinity named above. Our battle is and in this life will always be against the world, the flesh, and the devil.

The world has its agenda planned by the devil, who is

the god of this world (2 Cor. 4:4). He has set in motion a devious but brilliant and systematic plan. The world system works to destroy God's agenda.

Regarding the flesh, D. L. Moody said, "I have more trouble with D. L. Moody than any other person I know." Christians still have the flesh indwelling them, and it does not improve. The day a Christian dies, even if he or she is a mature saint, that Christian possesses the same potential in the flesh for evil that he or she had the day of conversion. Some Christians have the strange idea that somehow if we read enough of the Bible and sing enough hymns, we won't have the same capacity for evil that once resided in the deeper regions of our souls. This notion is both biblically and practically false; the internal battle is always there. However, the power of Christ to overcome is the new factor, and hopefully we make regular choices that enable it to control our lives.

The devil is active and doggedly determined to slow down and frustrate God's redemptive plan. Though he is a defeated foe, at present he is free to roam the universe to ply his trade.

Our greatest challenges to disciple making will always come from this unholy triad. We confront those challenges with the weapons of the finished work of Christ and a resurrected Christ. At the point of the battle is a supernatural clash between the forces of evil and God himself.

> Finally, be strong in the Lord and in his mighty power. Put on the full armor of God so that you can take your stand against the devil's schemes. For our struggle is not against flesh and blood, but against the rulers, against the authorities, against the powers of this dark world and against the spiritual forces of evil in the heavenly realms. Therefore put on the full armor of God, so that when the day of evil comes, you may be able to stand your ground.
>
> Ephesians 6:10–13

Part II

Reasons to Be Committed

5

People Need Big Reasons
● ●

One of my most vivid memories of the 1960s is a monk, seated in a meditative posture, setting himself on fire. What could be so important about political life that a person would do something like that? Other people went on hunger strikes, and still others burned their draft cards or their country's flag. More recently, protesting students in China risked their lives for the sake of political freedom. When we think of this incident, the picture frozen in most of our minds is the solitary student standing in the path of a tank and not willing to let it pass unless it ran him down.

History has no shortage of examples of those who have given their lives for a particular cause. The Middle East continues to serve up doses of death for those who consider their political cause more precious than life itself. It seems incongruent, even surreal, then, to hear a Christian who possesses the message of complete and final freedom to say, "I can't commit to a six-week group or to teaching a children's class."

What causes people to make total commitment? Whatever the reason, it is clear they do have reasons. Somehow they have a worldview that makes their sacrifice worth the risk.

If you analyze it, most people who make total commitments are either leaders who have processed the big picture or individuals who have been inspired by powerful leaders. That leader may be a Hitler, a Mao, or a Lenin, who built their houses on philosophical sand, but they put together the big picture and proceeded to inspire others to the cause.

People are "wired" by their Creator to gravitate to causes that are bigger than themselves, to give their lives ultimate meaning. The greatest need of humankind is for life to have meaning. *Foxe's Book of Martyrs* chronicles the lives of those whose philosophical houses were built on the solid rock of Jesus Christ. Even in our century, many have given their physical lives to maintain the integrity of their spiritual lives. This is still an inspiration to all who love and follow Christ, and we hope that his grace will be sufficient if we face similar decisions. As inspirational as the ultimate sacrifice has been to the starting and sustaining of movements, it takes more than the blood of martyrs to maintain a cause over a long period of time.

The Living Sacrifice

Some have stated that dying for Christ is easier than living for him. I wouldn't want to subscribe to an idea that is built on such a low view of sacrifice. How would anyone alive know how difficult it is to give your life?

I do know, however, that the church is built not only on the sacrifice of Christ, but also on his resurrection. The resurrection provides the power and reason to be a living sacrifice. "Therefore, I urge you, brothers, in view of God's mercy, to offer your bodies as living sacrifices, holy and pleasing to God—this is your spiritual act of worship" (Rom. 12:1).

People need a big reason to die for a cause, but they need just as penetrating a reason to live a sacrificial life. Dying for a spouse or child is instinctual, but being willing to extinguish our existence calls for a compelling motivation. Living for something requires a powerful and sustainable cause. I recall a statement of Malcolm Muggeridge with respect to sacrifice. After visiting with Mother Teresa and seeing her work in Calcutta, he wrote that he suddenly realized how deep was her dedication and how superficial was his. Whereas martyrdom requires a few moments of courage, living sacrificially calls for a daily denial of many of life's available pleasures.

A Life of High Commitment

An unknown writer said, "Anything less than a conscious commitment to the important is an unconscious commitment to the unimportant."

Many commit themselves to the unimportant by default. They may be highly committed, but they are committed to the wrong thing, the unimportant thing. They have not been challenged, inspired, or directed to the important. Because the important has not been made a viable option for them, their only choice has been to be committed to material gain and building their egos. They give themselves to their work and the pleasures and perks that increase the fun and enjoyment of life. Why should they do anything else? They haven't been presented with any options.

They must be presented with a compelling reason. Perhaps then they would choose to commit to the important. There is little more tragic than Christians who spill their lives needlessly onto the ground. Whatever the cost of following Christ, the price paid for not following him is higher, and watching people waste their lives is difficult. As a pastor, I could hardly stand to see people make decisions that made them prisoners to cultural values. They willingly placed themselves in positions where they were not able to say yes to God.

As Dallas Willard says:

> Nondiscipleship costs abiding peace, a life penetrated throughout by love, faith that sees everything in the light of God's overriding governance for good, hopefulness that stands firm in the most discouraging of circumstances, power to do what is right and withstand the forces of evil. In short, it costs exactly that abundance of life Jesus said he came to bring (John 10:10). The correct perspective is to see following Christ not only as the necessity it is, but as the fulfillment of the highest human possibilities and life on the highest plane.[1]

At first, commitment to the unimportant seems easier. There is generally less immediate suffering; you can get what the world has convinced you that you need. You think of self-denial as a distant virtue reserved for saints, something to be celebrated but not experienced. In the long term, however, commitment to the unimportant becomes extremely painful. Only near the end of their lives do many lament not spending enough time with their families. They look into history's rearview mirror and see a life littered with the temporary and empty. They gave themselves to those people who didn't really care about them and to projects that are long forgotten.

I often count the important people in my life as those who would be at my bedside in the last moments of life. The next would be those attending my funeral, and finally those who would care for the family I would leave behind. I tell pastors, "Your deathbed won't be surrounded by elders, deacons, and trustees. Don't sacrifice your family on the ecclesiastical altar." Having a false set of assumptions, followed by a false sense of priorities, will lead to a schedule that builds a house on the foundation of the unimportant.

In the Psalms, Asaph penned the most eloquent statement about the cost of nondiscipleship. With some bitterness he describes the apparent advantages and ease of life
experienced by those committed primarily to self. He
speaks of his own difficulty and pain in trying to do right.
Then he presents a glorious admission and revelation in
one statement, "When I tried to understand all this, it was
oppressive to me till I entered the sanctuary of God; then
I understood their final destiny" (Ps. 73:16–17). His song
concludes with a terrible truth: "Those who are far from
you will perish; you destroy all who are unfaithful to you"
(v. 27). Yes, for a non-Christian the cost of nondiscipleship
is eternal separation from God, in a place called hell.

For a Christian the cost of nondiscipleship is lack of
blessing both here and in eternity. It means a life of trouble that is nonproductive; suffering that is not redemptive;
and a life of wandering in the wilderness of personal rebellion. This leads to the first and foundational reason any
follower of Christ has for living a life of high commitment.

Why the Committed Life?

"You shall have no. . . ." "You shall not make. . . ." "You
shall not misuse. . . ." "You shall not murder, commit adultery, steal, lie, or covet." These are not suggestions to consider it, pray about it, or come to terms with it; they are
commands. Just do it! These are Ten Commandments, not
suggestions or recommendations that we get to vote on.
God knows nothing of focus groups in order to build a personal ownership of his commands. God is top down and
dogmatic. He violates our politically correct sensibilities.
This outlook may irk many who think that following Christ
is a team kind of thing in which Jesus and I talk things over
and determine what I should do. In some cases that might
be true, but not on the "big ticket" items—such moral codes
as the Ten Commandments and the clear imperatives of
Scripture.

What a marvelous church we would have if Christians simply read the Bible and did it! Yes, and parents say, "What marvelous families we would have if children simply obeyed their parents and did what they were told." But that is not the way earthly or spiritual children behave. It is the nature of children to learn the hard way.

As spiritual children of the heavenly Father, we should obey his commands in the same way that we expect our earthly children to obey our commands. Shouldn't this be the only reason we would ever need to be totally committed? Is it not enough to know we are doing our duty, being obedient to the One who bought us with his own blood, being submissive as a servant of the King? Of course, we should. It should be enough for us to pursue the committed life simply because God says so. But God, in his mercy, gives us additional reasons for obedience and speaks of the many benefits of the highly committed life.

Why Not Be Normal?

I have already stated that high commitment is the normal Christian experience. To be casual or partially invested in the church and its work is abnormal and pathological. Since casual Christianity is accepted and even rewarded in today's evangelical churches, our churches are abnormal and sick. What does it take to be normal?

The Stepford Wives, a sci-fi film from the mid-seventies, tells the story of the upper-middle-class community of Stepford. The men are mostly high-tech engineers and businessmen. All the wives are happy, fresh-faced homemakers, who relish being totally subservient to their husbands. They are ecstatic over sewing, cleaning, baking, and pleasing their husbands. They never fight with or are unpleasant to anyone. They have no opinions or interests beyond their families and city clubs. If a few are too feisty, they leave on vacation with their husbands and on returning are as focused on cookies and clean floors as the rest. When this happens to the best friend of the newest Stepford wife, she becomes very suspicious. Desperate to know the truth, she stabs her friend with a knife, to see if she bleeds; she doesn't! She merely repeats pathetic little maneuvers around her kitchen, mouthing the same phrases over and over, while her frightened friend backs away and turns to run out of the house.

When it comes to Christian disciplines, there is a real danger that well-meaning believers can become dutiful robots, people going through the motions of spirituality without the heartfelt passion that gives it life. But an even greater danger is the total neglect of duty and discipline. That is the danger into which modern evangelicals have fallen. We have sacrificed duty and discipline on the altar of relevance.

I would like us to return to a more historic view of spirituality. Because of the great hunger for depth among today's unsatisfied evangelicals, the term *spiritual formation* is regaining some prominence. The term is based on Galatians 4:19–20: "My dear children, for whom I am again in the pains of childbirth until Christ is formed in you, how I wish I could be with you now and change my tone, because I am perplexed about you!" The lifelong process of a Christian taking on the character of Christ is called spiritual formation. The concept implies that Christlikeness takes its own unique form in every obedient Christian.

That is what it means to be a normal Christian.

The Tug of War

Journalist Bill Moyers believes the struggle of the century is over what it means to be spiritual. This is certainly the case among evangelicals. Everyone from the apostle Paul to Pascal to contemporary writers like Richard Foster, Dallas Willard, Howard Snyder, and Eugene Peterson would argue that spiritual formation is a process that requires the practice of a standard set of disciplines that will lead to the formation of Christlike character. Historic spirituality says there are a set of nonnegotiable habits that are required and expected of every disciple. On the other hand, the contemporary church says, "No! Take what you like, whatever fits your temperament, whatever seems to meet your needs, and get your needs met. That is spiritual enough."

Eugene Peterson has blasted much of today's excuse for spirituality: "Shun all spirituality that does not require commitment. For spirituality without commitment is like sexuality without commitment: quick, casual, superficial, impersonal, and selfish." *Shun* means more than "ignore." It means to go out of your way to make sure people understand your personal disgust. Essentially Peterson's exhortation is to have nothing to do with cheap and easy discipleship that corrupts Christianity.

There are those who claim that practicing spiritual disciplines has no connection to spirituality or character. I believe they are wrong and that anything less than the high standards of Scripture poses a clear danger to them and to those they teach. What does Scripture say about the practice of a standard set of disciplines?

The Road to Christlikeness Is Discipline

Look at Paul's advice to Timothy: "Train yourselves to be godly. For physical training is of some value, but godliness has value for all things. . . . Command and teach these things. Don't let anyone look down on you because you are young, but set an example" (1 Tim. 4:7–8, 11–12). The exhortations to be an example and to command and teach these things are broader than discipline alone, but certainly they include the role of discipline in godliness. The word *train* is translated "discipline" in other English versions. We get the word *gymnastics* from this Greek root, in which the concepts of rigor and repetition are inherent.

Paul's letter to the Colossians amplifies this. In the context of developing spiritual maturity in all who are willing, he employs the words "labor," "struggling," and "powerfully works" (Col. 1:28–29). Becoming like Christ takes discipline and requires work, struggle, and labor.

Scripture is also clear that the spirit of the disciplines is the Holy Spirit. Some people today attack the ideas of discipline and duty, saying they smack of legalism or works. But there was no confusion in the minds of the biblical writers, for they understood the mystery of God working his will and power via our will. "For it is God who works in you to will and to act according to his good purpose" (Phil. 2:13).

Through the Spirit, God builds into his children the inclination to obey him. This is the "I want to please him" element. But our responsibility is to step out in obedience. By the Holy Spirit, the human disciplines of repetition and practice, via structure, are joined to his divine energy and blessing.

You can't be godly without discipline; repetition and the acquisition of productive habits are keys to the development of Christlikeness. We learn to order our souls the same way we master a math problem or play golf well. If discipline were easy, we wouldn't need the multimillion-dollar industries to help us do right. A willing army of therapists, support groups, twelve-step programs, and other strategies are attempting to structure people's lives or give them discipline. Structure is vital to that process. Aristotle said that habits made all the difference.

Having Self-control

Self-control—there it sits all alone at the end of the line of other wonderful virtues. Love, joy, peace, and even patience seem to get better press. The very last fruit of the Spirit is greatly desired but many consider it to be out of reach. That is why, when people start listing the fruit of the Spirit, it is generally referred to as "etc." Self-control is the loneliest of virtues. Like a five-carat diamond, everyone wants it, but few are willing to pay the price. That price is rigorous training within the context of willing accountability.

It may seem like an impossible quest, but the Christian possesses the secret key through the Holy Spirit. From the moment of spiritual birth, the Christian possesses the "ought to" from the Holy Spirit. Then the responsibility shifts to the believer to step out in loving obedience. By becoming involved in a serious Christian community, the Christian can find help in keeping his or her commitments. Believers help each other practice habits such as interaction with Scripture and development of a prayer life, which create self-discipline.

Strict Training

Discipline manifests itself in structured repetition. In athletics, we call it training. Every year professional athletes leave the warmth of their families and the comforts of their multimillion-dollar homes and check into a spartanlike college dorm. For a few weeks they break the normal patterns of their lives, subjecting themselves to heavy physical rigor that would cause the average person to expire. This experience, called training camp, creates an artificial environment that accelerates the mental and physical conditioning of the athlete, in preparation for the season. Athletes are forced to do what they don't want so they can achieve the success they so desperately desire. The irony is that even the professional athlete who knows what to do in order to be successful will not and cannot do it on his own. He requires the help of coaching and structure.

Why do wealthy athletes subject themselves to such strict training? Obviously, they desire to make more money, and they can't do that unless they perform well. They also want to be respected by their colleagues, as well as by sports fans, but most importantly they want to win a championship.

While money, prestige, and respect are significant motivators, the greatest rewards for the great champions are the dignity and self-respect that come with doing your best. The biggest rewards are intangibles. Five times in his athletic metaphors the apostle Paul refers to either the goal, crown, or prize. In Philippians he identifies that prize as knowing God and resurrection power, along with living a productive life for him. In his second letter to Timothy he speaks of the crown or prize as a reward for a faithful, focused life (2 Tim. 4:7–8). If our lives are guided by a compelling why, we will subject ourselves to extraordinary disciplines to reach our goals.

How Long Can I Keep This Up?

When it comes to spiritual development, some might question the validity of artificial environments. Did Paul mean to teach us that a Christian goes into a permanent form of an artificial spiritual-training-camp mode? If he did, many will choose not to enroll.

But metaphor is not a method! Paul says, "Everyone who competes in the games goes into strict training" (1 Cor. 9:25). Most of us can only spend so long in training camp, at the "fat farm," or in some kind of rehab center. These special environments provide a "jump start." The desired end is the acquisition of new habit patterns that create different results.

What are some of these artificial environments that can increase the spiritual productivity of the motivated Christian who wants to "run the race to win"? Meeting one-on-one or in a small group for an agreed-upon period of time is an artificial environment that can accelerate growth and firmly set in new thinking and behavioral patterns. But we never cease to need some form of structured help. It is a matter of length and intensity. Just as there is never a time when a competing athlete no longer needs coaching, the disciple always needs accountability and training. A group may choose to retreat for an intense weekend or a week or two in order to catapult into a project, but after returning home it will settle into weekly or biweekly meetings. The church needs to be laced with networks of structured accountability groups and relationships that help everyone keep their commitments to God. After a team breaks camp, they still practice, and though much of life returns to normal, they are in condition and are ready to reach their goals. Artificial environments are meant to help people make the transition into more successful patterns.

Normal Christians have a goal of godliness and are willing to live with discipline and self-control (1 Tim. 4:7; Gal. 5:23). They will commit themselves to strict training and artificially structured environments, which will assist them in the acquisition of habits of the heart that in partnership with the Holy Spirit will form the character of Christ in their lives (1 Cor. 9:24–27; Gal. 4:19). In time, they will reap a spiritual harvest in their personal lives and in their connection to the church (Gal. 6:7–9).

Preparation

The abnormal or average Christian does not reap such a harvest because, in part, he or she is not prepared not to sin. Generally, the typical evangelical lives a defeated life. Many ordinary sins, translated "areas of weakness," are allowed to dominate throughout life. Hebrews 12:1–2 exhorts us not to allow this to happen: "Let us throw off everything that hinders and the sin that so easily entangles, and let us run with perseverance the race marked out for us." This means we need to discard habits, relationships, and anything else that makes it easier to sin and hinders us from running a long-distance race.

The two categories are "everything that hinders" and "the sin that so easily entangles us." There are non-sin issues that slow us down and clear sins that not only slow us down but also bring us down. They consistently entangle us and shut down our effectiveness.

Not long ago I was speaking at a men's retreat in New England. I seasoned my messages with athletic stories in order to raise the conference's male bonding ratio. As I told several stories that over the years have experienced a metamorphosis from interesting, to legend, to folklore, to mythology, I was wearing my T-shirt with "The older I get the better I was" written across it. The problem with being a self-made legend is that many want to see the proof by witnessing a faint glimmer of the past on the basketball court. The more I talked during the men's retreat, the more requests I received to play in the afternoon four-on-four round-robin basketball tournament. I attempted to retire to my quarters for a nice afternoon nap. After all, this is what a "washed up" forty-seven-year-old athlete with bone spurs should do. My first mistake was to stop at the courts and watch the teams warm up. They were bad; at least, I thought they were. But they really wanted me to play, and I finally said okay. My mind knew what to do; it just had forgotten it was in a decaying body that would betray its cerebral dictates.

After we lost the first game, I told my team that I was warmed up. Of course at forty-seven, warmed up means washed up, done. After we lost the second game, I knew I had made a mistake, but the old competitive juices wouldn't let me publicly acknowledge this primal truth. The opponents were nice enough, but for some reason I entered a negative emotional state toward that stupid kid (thirtyish) who was obviously cheating on every play by scoring baskets and gobbling up rebounds and pounding me into submission. I began to get angry; my memory bank offered up a series of dirty tricks that I had perfected nearly twenty-five years earlier. They didn't work. By this time people were asking, "Are you okay?" and, "Sure you don't want to sit down?"

At this point my attitude went further into the nether regions, and I started what is called "talking trash." How does the frustrated Christian leader talk trash to the younger pastor who is cleaning his clock? Within the parameters of the Judeo-Christian ethic, of course. You know it's time to quit when you have to say, "You're lucky you didn't have to play against me twenty-five years ago!"

It didn't make any difference that day how much I wanted to win. My desire to win has never been stronger. But my desire was helpless in the face of my unpreparedness. I didn't have the capacity to win. The key was not my will to win; it was my will to prepare to win. The same is true of sin. It is not just my will *not* to sin; it is also my will to *prepare* not to sin.

Preparing not to sin is the practice of the spiritual disciplines in the power of the Holy Spirit, and that is what we will be talking about in the next chapter.

6

Ten Disciplines
of the Committed Christian

● ●

With the encouragement of the community of Christ and with the supportive structures it provides, the habits of the heart that form Christlike character in the believer open the door to spiritual liberation and spiritual power. The common or abnormal Christian wishes not to sin but sins often and repeatedly for a lack of spiritual character. He or she lives from crisis to crisis, much of it self-imposed, because that person has ignored God's principles. The normal or highly committed Christian lives a disciplined life in which the very structures facilitate obedience and impede sin.

The three primary dimensions to a normal Christian experience are conversing with God, denial of the flesh, and serving Christ and his church. By possessing the will to prepare not to sin, the highly committed disciple can excel in all three dimensions of the spiritual journey. As the dean of renewal writers, Elton Trueblood once wrote, "Discipline is the price of freedom."

How many spiritual disciplines are there? It depends on whom you ask. They number anywhere from the twelve wonderfully treated by Richard Foster in *Celebration of Discipline*, to the fifteen identified by Dallas Willard in *The Spirit of the Disciplines*. After tracking the history of disciplines and their practices, Willard groups the disciplines under two headings: disciplines of abstinence and disciplines of engagement. Under the disciplines of abstinence, he mentions solitude, silence, fasting, frugality, chastity, secrecy, and sacrifice. Under the disciplines of engagement, he lists study, worship, celebration, service, prayer, fellowship, confession, and submission.

Willard goes on to say,

> In shaping our own list of spiritual disciplines, we should keep in mind that very few disciplines can be regarded as absolutely indispensable for a healthy spiritual life and work though some are obviously more important than others. Practicing a range of activities that have a proven track record across the centuries will keep us from erring.[1]

The spiritual disciplines are not a grace of God themselves. They only make connection to God more likely and more often, until communing with God becomes a habit. Charles Spurgeon put it this way: "I must take care above all that I cultivate communion with Christ, for though that can never be the basis of my peace—mark that—yet it will be the channel of it."[2]

For this book, I have identified ten practices that fall under the three dimensions of the normal Christian experience.

Conversing with God

Calvin Miller wrote, "Mystics without study are only spiritual romantics who want relationship without effort." What so many forget is that many if not all of the "deeper

saints" were scholars first. Before people go d
spirit, they are required to go deep in the mind.
course, is the natural route that God prescribes. Our l
are transformed by the renewing of our minds. The key to
the Spirit-filled life is the acquisition of the mind of Christ
(Rom. 12:2; 1 Cor. 2:9–16).

Three disciplines center on conversation with God: interacting with Scripture, prayer, and silence and solitude.

Interacting with Scripture

Every Christian has a need for spiritual nourishment. Peter says, "Like newborn babes, crave pure spiritual milk, so that by it you may grow up in your salvation, now that you have tasted that the Lord is good" (1 Peter 2:2–3). A Christian cannot grow and develop into anything much without a proactive interaction with God's written revelation. Paul dogmatically stated that to Timothy, "All Scripture is God-breathed and is useful for teaching, rebuking, correcting and training in righteousness, so that the man of God may be thoroughly equipped for every good work" (2 Tim. 3:16–17). Without information and wisdom, a person cannot be trained or equipped to serve. The writer of Hebrews refers to the precision of God's Word to discern and sort out the muddled issues of the mental and emotional dimensions of our personalities: "For the word of God is living and active. Sharper than any double-edged sword, it penetrates even to dividing soul and spirit, joints and marrow; it judges the thoughts and attitudes of the heart. Nothing in all creation is hidden from God's sight" (Heb. 4:12–13). The flesh cannot hide from Scripture's incision; there are no secrets from God or his Word. Interaction with it on a regular basis is absolutely necessary. Without this training, no one can do effective ministry.

Your interaction with the Word can take place on different levels, and its intensity will be determined by your interests and gifts. Those levels include:

ng to the Word as it is taught from
e other medium, such as radio or

of Scripture.
d's Word.
ure. This is an acquired skill that can
over a period of time.

ched Word is important, but some stud-
at personal Scripture reading is a powerful for.. shaping values. Memorization of Scripture will help block the entrance of sin into the believer's
life. That person has Scripture readily available for medi-
tation. The ability to study Scripture is a learned skill that
develops over time and provides for a deeper understanding of God's Word.

Interaction with Scripture not only builds the mind of
Christ in us but also provides us with the necessary information to know what God thinks about us and what he
wants from us. In addition, it provides us with a worldview by which we can understand the redemptive drama
that whirls all around us.

This is the first and most important spiritual discipline.
If we do not faithfully and regularly interact with Scripture,
there is very little future for Christians. J. I. Packer says,

> If I were the devil, one of my first aims would be to stop
> folk from digging into the Bible. Knowing that it is the
> Word of God teaching men to know and love and serve the
> God of the Word, I should do all I could to surround it with
> the spiritual equivalent of pits, thorn hedges, and man
> traps, to frighten people off. . . . At all costs I should want
> to keep them from using their minds in a disciplined way
> to get the measure of its message.[3]

Regular interaction with Scripture lays the foundation
for a productive future. Some will relish long hours of

study, while others will find a daily fifteen minutes a major challenge. What makes the difference? Sometimes it's a matter of spiritual interest. But it may also be the expectation placed upon the person by his church or spiritual leaders. Other important factors should be considered as well, such as giftedness, educational background, occupation, and the basic RPMs at which a person lives. While the length and the depth of study are negotiable, the regular interaction is not.

Christians must not be totally dependent on someone else—even their own pastor—for their intake of scriptural food. Any dependence on others becomes unhealthy, over the long run, and leads to an "arm's length" relationship with God. A Christian who wants to grow strong must not be fed by osmosis.

Prayer

God wants to communicate with us, and we need to talk with God. Most often he communicates with us through his chosen instrument, the Bible.

We talk to him in several ways. We begin with (1) adoration or praise. This is followed by (2) confession of all known sin. Then we (3) thank him specifically for whatever seems appropriate. Finally, we get to go for what we want; that is called (4) supplication or petitions. The evangelical prayer life has been characterized by snappy acronyms like ACTS (taken from the above). Our prayers should often include the elements of ACTS, but we must avoid being legalistic about it. For many years I was locked in this prayer closet made with my own categorical hands.

Like many, I desired a more dynamic relationship with God. Like many, I was seriously searching for a deeper, more satisfying relationship in communicating with God. I know God speaks to us through Scripture, but is he limited to Scripture? Does he speak to us in other ways? In the

past many would not even think in any other terms. God
spoke to Noah, Abraham, Moses, and the prophets, why
not me?

My experience is that God speaks in combinations and
clusters, using many different means. Scripture, of course,
is primary, but God may also speak to us through conversation, counsel of others, circumstances, simple impressions, personal desire, and longevity of desire. He may use
a cluster of Scripture, circumstance, and desire to impress
us to take a new job or move to a different city. If we feel
impressed not to get on a plane or to pick up a hitchhiker
or call an old friend, my advice is to try responding to the
impression a few times and see how reliable these lean-
ings are. If they prove to be valuable ministry opportunities that otherwise would have been lost, then you are
learning to follow the leading of the Spirit. Paul indicates
that if we are sons of God we will be led effectively by the
Spirit of God (Rom. 8:14; Gal. 5:16).

THE "GUT REACTION"

Life gives us both hard and soft data. Because of our
propositional mentality, we tend to discard the soft data.
I fully support a commitment to propositional truth that
is built on a scriptural foundation. At the same time I have
a healthy respect for the "gut reaction" of a spiritually
mature believer. When Christians have spent many years
developing their walks with God, their emotions, attitudes,
and wisdom have been trained to discern good from evil
(Heb. 5:14). This makes their response to various events a
well-studied soft-data reaction. There is great validity in
this kind of data, if checked by the more reliable hard data
of Scripture.

Once God has laid the foundation for his directional
leadership, a normally silly thing can become profound.
When I was trying to decide whether to stay in the pas-
torate or start an international training network for church

leaders, God employed a number of methods to let me know his will. I had followed the clear dictates of obedience to the Great Commission and thought it right to attempt to help many churches instead of just one church at a time. God had used material written to speak to leaders and call the church back to its disciple-making roots. He seemed to be leading me in the direction of a training ministry. I had three offers by which I could obey this calling. I counseled with many respected colleagues and friends. My desire to enter the new ministry was enduring, yet I was hesitant. I was in a no-man's-land. I knew what to do but wasn't able to get there emotionally.

Then one evening I was returning home from a meeting. It was dark and the only landmarks to be seen were billboards illuminated by artificial lighting. In the darkness, I was praying about my future. Then in front of me loomed a huge billboard with three words scrolled across it: *Go for It!* That was all I needed. Something that silly had become profound. It gave me the push I needed to commit myself to a new life direction.

Whatever method God uses, we have the confidence that it is all fenced in by God's written revelation. I can have many impressions and desires that are quite selfish and destructive. If I believe that I should buy a new home yet am not giving to God's work, it's obvious the desire isn't coming from the Lord. God's Word has spoken. I should not buy the house at the expense of God's work. It wouldn't make any difference how long your desire for a relationship outside your marriage persisted, there never would come a time when acting on that desire would be right.

Where God's Word provides specific revelation, as in the examples above, you are called to obey. But God has not provided every detail of life in his Word. No, instead he offers a living relationship that requires interaction. No rubber stamp applies to every Christian's life. There is only one

way to discover how God wants to communicate and talk
with you—ask him! The hymn says, "He walks with me,
and he talks with me, and he tells me I am his own." Knowing Christ is a walking and talking dynamic relationship.

Silence and Solitude

The other discipline involves silence and solitude. There
is ample scriptural support for both. When Jesus went into
the wilderness to be tempted by the devil, he was under
the leadership of the Spirit of God. He spent forty days in
solitude in that bleak wilderness. That is certainly longer
than normal, but considering the stakes of the confrontation ahead of him, it wasn't too long at all. Some time later,
Mark records that it was a regular pattern of Jesus to rise
early for time alone with his Father. In the Old Testament
even the lamentation over the death and destruction of
Jerusalem, penned by Jeremiah, speaks of the value of solitude: "It is good for a man to . . . sit alone in silence" (Lam.
3:27–28).

To stop talking and start listening to God is adventure
on the high seas, in uncharted waters, for evangelicals. For
most of us, listening to God has meant reading Scripture,
taking in a sermon, or listening to our parents. But when
we talk about spiritual disciplines, listening has a far more
profound meaning. In this case listening means allowing
God to work his mystery in us through our silent time
alone with him. I must admit that I am still working on
this, but recently I have been attempting to do more listening while being alone with God. I have yet to hear an
audible voice or any clear direction. Too often, common
thoughts rush through my mind at such times; I think of
daily jobs and responsibilities that must be accomplished.

It is beneficial, I believe, to link solitude and silence.
There are certainly benefits gained in retreating from normal life patterns. We live in a world of busy routine. Rou-

tine is a key to success. Unless we develop good habits and learn to live by them, we won't get too far in life. The negative, however, is that at times God finds it difficult to break into our routine long enough to speak to us and shape our attitudes. The benefit of intentionally separating ourselves from daily routine and from contact with people is to clear our heads and give God an opportunity. The very idea of being quiet, regardless of how unproductive it may seem at the time, is a part of the submission of our will. When the structural support system is removed, it challenges us to be alone with our thoughts.

I recently learned more about the debilitating effects of Alzheimer's disease. I'm learning that an important part of relating to someone with this disease is learning how to converse with him or her. It's like learning a different language because traditional ways of communicating may not be effective. How to read the person and understand what is going on is a learned skill. It is very frustrating for those of us accustomed to normal discourse to enter into this very different world.

Listening to God can be equally frustrating. God forbid that we should be so insecure that we have to fabricate God's speaking to make us feel good about ourselves. Frankly, God has told me enough for a lifetime, but I hunger for a more dynamic relationship, including more communication from him. I honestly am not expecting an audible voice or some apparition. I would, however, like to read better the impressions of the Spirit and more subtle forms of communication. For that reason, I will continue to come apart from daily routine and retreat to the heart of God.

Denials of the Flesh

We need to take part in the disciplines that make up our conversation with God, but talking with God and knowing his will are not sufficient for forming a mature spiritual life. Christians must also say no to those things that hinder spiritual maturity.

Before we look at the second major discipline, let's put a Scripture in our thinking:

> Dear friends, I urge you, as aliens and strangers in the world, to abstain from sinful desires, which war against your soul. Live such good lives among the pagans that, though they accuse you of doing wrong, they may see your good deeds and glorify God on the day he visits us.
>
> 1 Peter 2:11–12

I hope you still remember how we are defining normal. It is normal, by God's definition, for believers to converse with him through a variety of means. It is just as normal for them to deny themselves pleasure and perks that would hinder their witness and their work. For that reason I propose that denial is a prerequisite to the fullness of God.

What I didn't say was that it was the *only* prerequisite, just as I would not propose that self-discipline is the only important attribute to godliness. Both, however, are necessary, along with some other disciplines, to make a mature follower of Christ. Most people today consider self-denial as an old-fashioned value that belongs in the Smithsonian as a reminder of what made America great; it served our country and society well in the past, but it no longer plays a vital role. Those who believe such hooey are completely out of touch with human nature and what makes the world work. For the Christian, nothing is more necessary for fulfillment and happiness than self-denial. Paul brilliantly combines the Spirit-filled life and self-denial: "So I say, live by the Spirit, and you will not gratify the desires of the flesh" (Gal. 5:16). Obviously, the Spirit-filled life is not at home with unchecked pleasure.

Spiritual development is not automatic. It is not a passive flowing of God's power through our hearts and minds as we sit twiddling our thumbs. Why do I say this? Because "the sinful nature desires what is contrary to the Spirit, and the Spirit what is contrary to the sinful nature. They are in conflict with each other, so that you do not do what you want" (Gal. 5:17).

Wanting something does not mean I need it or that I should get it. Oscar Wilde said there were two tragedies in life. One was not getting what you want, and the second was getting it. In getting what they want, many become slaves to society's mythology that we deserve what we want but cannot have. Learning to say no to self in order to say yes to God is indeed a prerequisite for fulfillment. As Bob Dylan sang, "You Gotta Serve Somebody." The Christian can serve self or God. Most people serve self and thus are slaves to self and sin. Their flesh dominates their lives, and personal peace and fulfillment are distant dreams, mostly daydreams. The Christian says no to those things he wants that are clearly sin and also says no to those desires that compete with God's purpose. Some would call this legalism, but Paul certainly didn't. "But if you are led by the Spirit, you are not under law" (Gal. 5:18).

Under the heading of self-denial, I would list three spiritual disciplines: fasting, frugality, and sacrifice.

Fasting

Saying no to the body is a challenge. For most of us denying ourselves something so naturally attractive and good as food is a negative. Not only do we miss the smells and tastes, but intense hunger creates discomfort. However, the discomfort reminds us that we are doing something sacrificial and causes us to focus on prayer. This is not a book or even a treatise on fasting; my only point is that fasting is a practice that reveals our serious commitment to God.

Frugality

Saying no to materialism is antithetical to our culture. I have counseled many Christians whose commitment to materialism has kept them from obedience to God. Making good decisions concerning the accumulation of wealth and things is essential to giving God an opportunity to direct us in his ways. If I cannot answer God's call because of material ownership or obligations, then I have erred.

I like what Urban T. Holmes III says about this tension:

> Mortification is the intentional denial of legitimate pleasures in the spirit of Christian poverty that one might become more human. In my tradition Lent has long been considered a time for mortification, although one would not use such a medieval word. We gave up eating desserts, going to movies, or telling dirty jokes, all of which in the face of world problems seemed rather trivial. Once revered silly, we dismissed the idea of giving up and talked of taking on. What we failed to understand was that a life incapable of significant sacrifice is also incapable of courageous action.[4]

How significant this could be in finding the contemporary "missing link" that makes long-term, high commitment a rare evangelical commodity! Because we practice self-denial so seldom, commitment is too much for our flabby wills. Our characters are underdeveloped, our wills are weak, and our consciences are feeble—if not seared.

Evelyn Underhill writes, "Mortification means killing the very roots of self-love; pride and possessiveness, anger and violence, ambition and greed in all their disguises, however respectable those disguises may be, whatever uniforms they wear."[5]

Both fasting and frugality are important exercises in the development of the character of Christ and development of the ability to take definitive action to advance the kingdom of God. There is a link between the ability to say no to self and to say yes to God.

Sacrifice

I call it sacrifice when we say no to status, glamor, and luxury. This third area is closely related to the previous two. It may be a bit more intangible, however.

Sacrifice strikes at the root of the attitude that most hinders our spirituality—pride. Nothing gets in the way of God in our lives any more than pride. "God opposes the proud but gives grace to the humble. Humble yourselves, therefore, under God's mighty hand, that he may lift you up in due time. Cast all your anxiety on him because he cares for you" (1 Peter 5:5–7).

At the same time it is quite possible for us to become proud of our acts of self-denial. We see this all around us in modern society. The quest to be all you can be by taking that fascinating trip to ME has found its place in the pantheon of societal gods. Christians are not exempt from entering into this quest, though most make some effort to give it a spiritual label.

THE EVANGELICAL VERSION OF EGOTISM

"Be everything God wants you to be. . . ." "Discover your gift and use it. . . ." "Find your niche. . . ." "Work in your area of strength, not weakness." I have employed all these phrases. They all are harmless—even helpful when held in proper balance. The danger is their close relationship to our psychologized society. The question is, What is driving the quest, and in the final analysis, what governs our choices?

Some Christians reject God's call or turn down an opportunity because it's not in their area of giftedness or strength. Many well-intentioned teachers say that obedience to Christ always brings the believer peace and satisfaction. If God is in it, they teach, the work will be pleasant and problem free. But I have to ask: Is our quest for God's best simply an ego trip to build our self-esteem, or are we willing to take the diversions that God builds into our life's journey in order to strengthen our character?

Earlier in my life I wanted to move into a pastoral position. I had worked effectively as a volunteer youth leader, and the pastor wanted to add me to his staff. I had good experience but no formal training beyond an undergraduate degree. At the time I was working with a mission organization.

The church was scheduled to vote on my position on a Sunday evening. There didn't seem to be a doubt in anyone's mind that I would receive a call from this congregation. However, I was blissfully ignorant of the internal pressures in the church. I was not at all aware of the fact that my pastor was under a great deal of pressure not to hire me.

The day before the church business meeting, he informed me that the entire plan was off and that I should seek some other avenue of service. I was shocked. I had gone out on a limb. I had resigned my job with the mission organization. I wondered, *What am I going to do now?*

The answer was to swallow my pride and ask to return to the mission organization. When I did this, the mission asked me to move to another city, and that meant attendance at a different church, where a part-time position became available, along with an opportunity for graduate education.

God disappointed my immediate expectations in order to enhance and improve my future ability to minister. I was in the wrong city, the wrong denomination, and without proper theological education. I had been sure that I was supposed to remain where I was, but God knew better.

For most of us the challenge is to submit our view of God's best to God for his appraisal of what is best. This calls for saying no to self, for submitting our plans to him, and even delaying the implementation of deeply held convictions. Self-denial is an important step to saying yes to God. Many Christians today, unpracticed in the delay of gratification, are consequently prisoners of their own unchecked appetites. For those who can't say no to their bodies, who can't say no to the accumulation of wealth, and who can't say no to the feeding of their egos, there is little chance to make a commitment to Christ.

Serving Christ and His Church

The third grouping of spiritual disciplines strikes the Christian character in a most practical arena. These issues are spiritual authority, financial stewardship, willingness to be trained, and personal evangelism. At this juncture many of us separate from our theology. In other words, do we practice the disciplines that lead to spiritual strength or, after a courteous nod to our theology, do we go on to secular solutions and strategies?

A clear proposition that is not mentioned enough is that you can't have Christ without also having his church. A Christian cannot be anything close to God's creative plan for him without activity in the church. Many think they can be their own church. But Augustine wisely said, "He cannot have God for his father who does not have the church for his mother."

Church membership is not optional. Martin Luther said "Apart from the church, salvation is impossible." This does not mean that the church provides salvation. Rather it means that you can't fulfill what it means to be a disciple of Christ apart from the local church, so membership is the mark of salvation. Every regenerate disciple is already a part of the church. Then the exhortation of Scripture is to find the local manifestation of the church that fits you. To say that you can't find that right church is an unacceptable excuse. If God expects it, he will provide the direction for you. It won't be perfect, and it might not cater to your immediate felt needs, but still that is no reason to disobey God.

"And let us consider how we may spur one another on toward love and good deeds. Let us not give up meeting together, as some are in the habit of doing, but let us encourage one another—and all the more as you see the Day approaching" (Heb. 10:24–25). The Christian who does not attend church is an incomplete Christian. There is no real possibility that God's plan for one's life can be reached without church attendance. The disciple will miss the dynamics of interpersonal relationships, not only with those he or she likes, but with those he or she may dislike.

The first step in discipleship is to help a Christian enter into the church. Basic follow-up, as it is known, will be of very little use until this is done. The church helps us accept others, it is reality therapy, it gives us the big picture and the importance of the global mission. There are no commands in Scripture for non-Christians to go to church; however, there are several exhortations for the believer to do so. After a Christian has become part of a church, he should seek areas of service.

According to the primary passages on the church in the New Testament, the church is pictured as a gifted team that works together for the overall benefit of its members. If we accept these passages (Rom. 12:1–9; 1 Cor. 12; Eph. 4:11–16), we must accept the responsibility to work in the church.

Every Christian is given at least one spiritual gift. The responsibility that goes with it is made very clear by the apostle Peter. "Each one should use whatever gift he has received to serve others, faithfully administering God's grace in its various forms. If anyone speaks, he should do it as one speaking the very words of God. If anyone serves, he should do it with the strength God provides, so that in all things God may be praised through Jesus Christ" (1 Peter 4:10–11).

Serving others so God gets the credit: That is the attitude that makes the church work. Spirit-controlled disciples exhibit selfless service. "Submit to one another out of reverence for Christ" (Eph. 5:21). Good Christians become part of the church in order to serve, for the benefit of others and for the glory of God. They develop their gifts and use them as offerings to God, to help the greater good. When done with a positive attitude, these actions are partial proof of the filling of the Holy Spirit (Eph. 5:17–21). The normal Christian is to be a servant of Christ in and through the church; anything less is aberrant and disobedient.

Spiritual Authority

A vital link that helps Christians serve is their acceptance of spiritual authority. "Obey your leaders and submit to their authority. They keep watch over you as men who must give an account. Obey them so that their work will be a joy, not a burden, for that would be of no advantage to you" (Heb. 13:17).

Lay aside for a moment any controversy over how a local church leader derives authority. The issue is that all Christians are members of the universal church and thus are called to work this out by membership in its local manifestation. We are helped in keeping our commitments to God through the wise application of spiritual authority in the context of that local body.

One of evangelicalism's anomalies is a high view of secular authority and a low view of spiritual authority. Most evangelicals consider praying for elected officials a part of their sacred calling. They teach their children to salute the flag and to love their country. However, Christian parents who may discipline their children for showing disrespect to their country may also criticize and undermine the authority of their pastor in front of the children. They may ignore the decisions of their church leaders and feel no obligation to go along with their leadership. One reason for disrespect of spiritual leadership is that people experience no immediate consequences for doing it.

Financial Stewardship

I personally believe in tithing. Giving 10 percent off the top of our possessions preceded even the law of Moses. Giving 10 percent off the top symbolizes God's ownership of all my material wealth. According to Malachi 3:8–12, anyone who does not bring a tithe to the Lord's work is a thief. Not only does failure to tithe rob God, the person who cheats God is also denied the wonderful spiritual and material benefits of giving. You can't steal from God without his knowing it, and the results can last for eternity. When you fail to give, you also rob God's work of its ability to advance around the world.

The New Testament gives additional instruction:

> Remember this: Whoever sows sparingly will also reap sparingly, and whoever sows generously will also reap generously. Each man should give what he has decided in his heart to give, not reluctantly or under compulsion, for God loves a cheerful giver. And God is able to make all grace abound to you, so that in all things at all times, having all that you need, you will abound in every good work.
>
> 2 Corinthians 9:6–8

There is liberty in the whole issue of giving. It begins with a rule of thumb that God expects a minimum of 10 percent, off the top, as an act of faith and allegiance. Then there are offerings that exceed the 10 percent. These are given thoughtfully, as prompted by the Holy Spirit, in keeping with a person's resources (1 Cor. 16:2). God leads people to make special gifts that are above the 10 percent. If you would ask me to rate a disciple who never exceeds the 10 percent, I would simply say he is not listening to God, because in the course of a year God will certainly prompt us to make special gifts. Why would any intelligent believer lock himself out of such multiple blessing?

Some say all the tithe goes to the local church, bec
it is the equivalent of the storehouse mentioned in Mal
3:8–10. But I think that is a huge exegetical leap. I beli
that God's work can be a local church or any evangeli
cause that is supported and blessed by local churches. Our
first dollars should go to the place where we get our spiritual training and encouragement and where our family is
being ministered to. Your local church is where you have
chosen to invest time and energy as well as submit to
spiritual leadership, and that is where your first dollars
should go.

However, one trend that continues to erode the ability
of the local church to function is the increase of giving to
parachurch ministries instead of to the local church. As a
pastor, I asked members to give at least half of their tithe
to the church and certainly no less than that. Members
should do whatever is necessary to make their church a
success, because it is the best instrument to reach and minister to people of every stage of life and spiritual development. I support parachurch works; they have been wonderfully used by God, and they often target specific needs
that the church cannot address. The church, however, is
much broader in its appeal on the local level.

Willingness to Be Trained

It makes no sense for a person to join a church but not
submit to options for spiritual development. In fact, every
serious Christian has a responsibility to God and the
church to discover his or her spiritual strength and use it
for the benefit of others (1 Peter 4:10–11). The task of spiritual leaders is to "prepare God's people for works of service, so that the body of Christ may be built up" (Eph. 4:12).
That purpose statement in Ephesians is immediately followed by the importance of transformation from spiritual
childhood to spiritual maturity. The exhilarating finish of

the paragraph claims that only when Christians are trained and grow can they be productive. "From him the whole body, joined and held together by every supporting ligament, grows and builds itself up in love, *as each part does its work*" (Eph. 4:16, italics mine). Every Great Commission church is committed to training every member. That is the right and productive thing to do. Any Christian who does not desire to be trained must have his or her commitment to Christ, even the reality of his or her profession of faith, challenged.

There may be times when the struggling will be stagnated and those just seeking God may not be ready for a training experience. The objective is to create the expectation that being trained to be the best Christian possible, who will reap a great harvest, is normal. Again the issue becomes not whether every member is a serious Christian, but whether the leaders are modeling a willingness to be trained. Everyone should understand that this is what is esteemed and honored in the church. If someone is not eager to be trained, especially the more seasoned saint, it is very likely that person's heart has grown cold and he or she is suffering from the root sin of pride.

Personal Evangelism

Is sharing one's faith normal? I believe that personal witness is crucial to spiritual development. So many people, even leaders, spend their lives serving Christ but leaving out the most joyous of all experiences, telling others about their spiritual journey. Can you imagine never talking about your spouse or children? It would be absurd to even consider such a possibility for it violates human nature not to talk about life's passionate relationships. And our most passionate relationship should be the one we have with Christ.

It is imperative to get new believers started soon on personal storytelling. This may sound cynical, but it is important to get new Christians sharing their faith as a normal activity before more seasoned saints tell them that most people don't really do that. This attitude is often taught by example. I have stated it before but here goes one more time. Without evangelism, our Bible study becomes academic, our prayer lives boring, and our fellowship superficial. Evangelism is the catalyst for the spiritual disciplines. It brings life to the other dimensions of the Christian experience, and helps us understand when we are not participating in the mission of Christ to the world.

When I leave home each day my prayerful discipline is to ask God to give me an opportunity to represent him well that day. When he gives me an opportunity, the spiritual discipline is to take advantage of it, regardless of how I feel. I may think myself too busy or I may be in an angry or selfish mood. There is always the temptation not to tell others. I know that being disciplined to obey is going to bear fruit. Part of that fruit will be my own spiritual development and self-respect.

A Metaphor from the Garden

Eugene Peterson has given us a useful metaphor from gardening that helps us all understand the value and use of spiritual disciplines. In his challenging work, *Under the Unpredictable Plant: An Exploration in Vocational Holiness*, he likens our souls to soil. Just as the soil has a constant need for water and sun, our souls constantly need God's Word and prayer. Those are the daily needs of the soul. If we were, however, required to practice all the disciplines simultaneously, it would be a sure formula for failure. The other disciplines, such as solitude, fasting, and sacrifice, he likens to gardening tools that are nearby and used periodically to make sure the soil is free of weeds and is cultivating growth as it should.

All the disciplines are essential to spiritual health, but each must be applied at the proper time, under the guidance of God's Spirit. None of the disciplines can be abandoned without harming the spiritual life.

Too few Christians are committed to the regular practice of spiritual disciplines. Much too often the consistent practice of the spiritual disciplines outlined in this chapter is considered a reason for sainthood. God says, no way; these disciplines are expected from any Christian who wants to be considered a normal follower of Christ.

7

The Fulfilled Life

In our low-commitment world, fulfillment is an oft-sought after but rarely found commodity. People search for something more but many never reach the end of their quest, because they become mired in an undemanding lifestyle that will not disrupt their ways of thinking and acting.

Still, deep down, every person longs to know that his or her life really means something. We see that desire in the causes that people are willing to die for. Whether it's saving babies, trees, or whales, those engaged in such causes find that they give meaning to their lives.

Jesus calls normal Christians to a life of greater promise and deeper fulfillment than any of these causes can promise. But before Christians set out, Jesus tells them to look ahead and understand the cost of the committed life.

Counting the Cost

What will it cost me if I do this? is the question that measures the cost of discipleship. *What will happen if I don't do this?* measures the cost of nondiscipleship. Whatever discipleship's cost, it is less than that of nondiscipleship. Choosing not to follow Christ costs a person eternity. Though following him may be at times tougher in the here and now, that trouble is fleeting; it is a light affliction in comparison to the eternal weight of the glory that will someday be ours (2 Cor. 4:14–16).

Counting the cost requires some long-range strategic thinking; you are required to make a number of major decisions. Jesus talked about this subject in Luke 14:25–35. Just as a man building a tower estimates the cost before he begins building, even so disciples of Christ should understand the costs involved.

Every Person Must Do It

Luke 14 is often taught as a high-commitment passage that is only for the serious Christian. Supposedly, only seasoned Christians are ready to hear such stiff standards. That interpretation is more sociologically than exegetically based. What today's evangelical culture calls normal Jesus considers disobedient. When Jesus spoke these words, he called on "anyone" traveling in the "large crowds." The requirements of discipleship are requirements for every follower. There are no escape clauses for the too busy, the overworked, or even new believers.

Jesus' next statement has created a kaleidoscope of responses. Some write it off as fable; others have employed it as an excuse to neglect their families; most throw up their hands and admit, "I don't know what it means."

"If anyone comes to me and does not hate his father and mother, his wife and children, his brothers and sisters— yes even his own life—he cannot be my disciple" (Luke 14:26). My understanding of the passage is that, in comparison to my dedication to Christ, my devotion to others is so distant that it might seem like hate. I do believe Jesus is using hyperbole in the statement. Many biblical directives tell us to love our spouses and children, so we cannot take the plain meaning of these words (Deut. 6:1–4; Prov. 22:6; Eph. 5:21–6:4, for example). Jesus is simply saying, "I'm first; I will have no rivals." Putting Christ first must be normative for every Christian. Because the cost is high, we are exhorted to think very carefully before saying yes.

Avoid Disgrace—Be a Finisher

Jesus gives two examples of counting the cost, building a tower and engaging in war. With these, we can easily understand that Christians have a responsibility to carefully calculate what a commitment will mean in time, money, effort, and its effect on others important to us. Lack of attention to this principle creates tremendous hurt in the church when a believer fails to follow through. The passage puts it well: "This fellow began to build and was not able to finish." Ridicule for not being able to finish a task is tough for anyone to take, but Jesus tells us that it can be avoided.

This passage speaks not only to the decider, but also to the recruiter. People need full disclosure regarding the work they are being asked to do. Too much "bait and switch" has become part of what is called the "recruiting wars" or the free-for-all competition for the faithful few. When workers find out that many more, or entirely different, talents are required than were originally advertised, they feel used and betrayed. If the position or work is not carefully crafted, they feel used; and they feel betrayed if the cost is higher and the journey longer than reported. The best possible scenario is for the recruiter to lay out the vision and fully disclose the nature of the work. Actually this makes the work more inviting. You don't want the people who are looking for the easy, quick, and unimportant. Such would-be disciples don't count the cost—they count the minutes until they are done. The decider's task is to carefully consider the work and what it will mean in time and energy. If this is done, you end up with more fulfilled workers who finish strong and well.

Making the Payments

In the previous passage on counting the cost, Jesus addresses a large crowd. However, in Luke 9:23–25, Jesus gives additional teaching on discipleship, and here the audience is the twelve, those whom he had chosen to be with him so that they could go out and preach (Mark 3:14). The core teaching of both passages is the same, but each has its own personality. Because of their similarities, I conclude that, although only the twelve are listening here, the teaching is for the broader populace. The Luke 14 passage tells us to consider the long-range, strategic factors in following Jesus; Luke 9 takes us into the trenches of everyday life.

The basic teaching is that we must deny ourselves, when whatever else we want gets in the way of obedience. Just as it was at the heart of Christ's redemptive mission, the cross represents my mission. The cross is not a negative symbol; rather, it represents a disciple's primary life task— that specific work that God has called us to. Though ours could be a difficult task, much of the time it could be very pleasant. The cross symbolizes that unavoidable mission we must undertake to be obedient.

In this passage in Luke 9 Jesus seems to emphasize the word "daily." The disciple must "take up his cross daily and follow me" (Luke 9:23). If counting the cost is the initial strategic decision, then daily denial of self-interest is the process of making the payments on that cost. Every morning and throughout the day we make the same decision many times. This does not get easier as we grow older; the flesh is quite deceptive and creates new and interesting temptations as we age. When we are young, the adrenaline runs powerfully through our veins, presenting a series of obvious temptations that don't require cataloging. In middle age the adrenaline flow lessens, but our efforts to retain our vigor and youth encourage many deleterious and foolish actions. The golden years bring new and frustrating physical challenges, impatience with the young, and sometimes bitterness, along with a judgmental spirit. Saying no to self is an unnatural act at any age; it is, however, a supernatural decision. What do you get for a lifetime of such submission of your will to the ministry and leading of the Holy Spirit?

The Promise for the Highly Committed

If you want to save it, then lose it. That is certainly strange advice for our keep-it, hide-it, lock-it-up world. Yet clearly Scripture teaches us that everything precious in life cannot be kept unless it is offered to God first as a love offering.

Christ promises that by giving our lives to him we will have these priceless characteristics that make us rich in eternal goods: inner peace, fulfillment, and a sense of purpose and significance. The down side is that if we choose any other way we forfeit life's greatest rewards. The simple fact is, unless we enter discipleship on God's terms, he flatly tells us it isn't discipleship.

The church is largely populated with undiscipled disciples who have decided not to follow Jesus, and the double tragedy is that leaders have said it is okay. Not all leaders have collapsed under the weight and pressure of culture to let up on the saints. But plenty of corrupted evangelical theology permits inferior standards to be considered discipleship, even in the face of all that Jesus has declared. Jesus says that kind of disciple is not submitting himself to discipleship, so don't call it that and don't expect the rewards that go with discipleship. Life is daily, and so is discipleship. We must take up our mission daily and follow him.

If we obey, the rewards are wonderful.

An Interest-Bearing Account

When Jesus taught that riches were a serious hurdle to getting to heaven, Peter responded, "We have left everything to follow you." Jesus answered with a wonderful promise, "I tell you the truth, no one who has left home or brothers or sisters or mother or father or children or fields for me and the gospel will fail to receive a hundred times as much in this present age (homes, brothers, sisters, mothers, children and fields—and with them persecutions) and in the age to come, eternal life" (Mark 10:28–30).

I'm not going to tackle the "sticky parts" of the promise. I am sure he is not promising to replace your genetic family with a spiritual family. My hunch is that he will provide the committed Christian who must leave behind these things with emotional and physical compensation of some kind. The aspect that I want to emphasize is the promise of a hundredfold return on our original investment. Jesus promised some dividend in this life, and the payments continue for eternity. The positive aspect of discipleship is the promise—and such rewards will be given only to those who do make sacrifices.

In all three passages there is a clear stream of teaching that the highly committed, normal Christian will receive tremendous benefit both here and now and for all eternity.

Jesus taught that

1. Long-range, strategic thinking and calculation of cost, so we can finish well.
2. A daily requirement to actualize that long-term commitment in concrete decisions.

3. The commitment to make significant sacrifice will be returned to us a hundred times over.

When we follow the example of Christ and present the call to discipleship in the same way he did, we can also be assured that those who make commitments in response to that challenge will receive:

- purpose, peace, and meaning
- excellent work that is finished
- the thanks and the honor of God
- satisfaction and fulfillment and a sense of accomplishment
- multiplied benefits in this life and for eternity
- avoidance of a trivial, pleasure-driven life that ends up a waste

No doubt those who have made a high, long-term commitment have experienced such benefits and can challenge others to a life of discipleship; but once the Spirit has convicted people to take the path of discipleship, how do we build them up in the committed life?

That is the focus of our next two chapters.

Part III

How to Build and Keep Commitment

8

Seven Steps
That Build High Commitment

Agreed, Christians intensely struggle for commitment, and people need reasons to make high commitment. But God doesn't expect us to achieve high commitment strictly from a posture of duty. While duty plays a part, the Designer of human personality knows how to tap in to our motivation. The spiritual battle rages because the enemy opposes our commitment to God.

Ironically Christians resist what they actually want. We all have a "factory-installed" need to please and obey God. Unless we have layered it over by years of inaction, many of us even long for a highly committed life.

The first half of the book acknowledged these realities; now we move to the action points. Parts one and two have dealt with the struggle for and reasons why the normal Christian should live a life of high dedication to God. After that decision has been made, the following seven steps to building and sustaining high commitment should be taken by the individual and the corporate leadership of the church.

Step 1: Create a High-Commitment Environment

High commitment is a message for the multitudes. That means it's for everyone. We have looked at several high-commitment passages that support this thesis. In Luke 9:23–25; 9:57–62; and 14:26, high commitment is for "anyone who would follow me" or "come after me." The teaching of Luke 9:57–62 springs from a statement made by an unidentified man along the road. While the 9:23–25 passage setting only involves the twelve, the teaching is for "anyone" and is consistent with Jesus' other requirements for following him. Jesus is telling us that while many of today's evangelical Christians may be Christians, they are really less Christian than he requires.

While it is a message for everyone, in all candor I must admit that only a few make high commitment a practiced reality. Why? I believe this is because evangelical pastors have not presented it as the norm, for fear of being too hard or not loving or not user-friendly enough. Earlier I wrote, "the contemporary evangelical church environment works against high commitment." This is the "itching ears" syndrome. Paul warned Timothy that some would reject sound doctrine and gather their favorite teachers around them to tell them what they want to hear (2 Tim. 4:3–4). By the advertisers, the demographers, pundits, and pollsters evangelical pastors have been sold a "bill of goods." They have been told that the way to reach people is to start with what the people want to hear and think they need.

What a coup for the enemy! Evangelicals listen to what corrupted minds and damaged spirits of a fallen culture tell us about the needs of people. The mind is sick, deceptive, and desperately wicked; who can know it? the Scripture asks. The answer is that only God really understands our needs and knows what the content of the message should be. The attitude of the communicator is the determining factor. Don't back off on the truth of the message, but back off on the judgmental spirit and any self-righteousness in the message.

How do we create a high-commitment environment without blasting the seekers and the sensitive out of the pew?

Preach It from the Pulpit

The pastor's primary role is to faithfully set the standard for what it means to be a Christian. The pastor defines normal; he tells the congregation what it means to be a disciple. People need an expectational level to which they can aspire. In a church setting, those already highly committed will reach for the standard of behavior set by the pastor. The more it is esteemed and honored, the more others will aspire to it.

A simple example is the expectation that every disciple is expected to faithfully represent Christ in our culture, in both word and deed. In some church environments people would say that every Christian should verbally witness; in others it would be diluted to witnessing by the quality of life alone. There is nothing quite as wrong and presumptuous as the notion that my walk with God by itself can bring anyone to Christ. As the late Sam Shoemaker stated, "It says too much about us and too little about Him." How the personal responsibility to witness is taught and then practiced in a church determines both how many do it and the number of conversions that the church experiences.

Another crucial issue is the standard chosen for congregational members in relation to the practice of certain spiritual disciplines. How high they set that standard reveals their theology. I am not speaking here of the trivialization of theology in saying, "We don't dance, go to movies, play cards, or have any real fun."

Some pastors see no relationship between inductive study and the commitment to memory of the Scriptures and spirituality. They would simply say that some regular interaction with the Word is sufficient. It could be discussing it at the small-group level, listening to radio preaching, or taking notes during a sermon. The former requires self-discipline; the latter two are done with others. Granted, spiritual wiring makes a difference, but it seems to me that both/and is the order of the day, not either/or. It is simply impossible for a person to be as godly without discipline (1 Tim. 4:7). Some good can be done by group activities, but often opting for this approach fosters an undisciplined life that leads to an "arm's length" walk with God.

What is best? To have a casual, incomplete understanding of God's work and methods or to really have it fixed in the mind and spirit? Everyone knows which is superior and what the standard should be. The ultimate answer is to set the standard where Scripture does, to do so with a positive affirming spirit, and to leave it at that. Don't succumb to the tendency to shrink back from the scriptural standard. Don't go beyond it, but don't lower it. If you do, God won't honor it, and people will not aspire to it.

When it comes to listening to preaching, people are amazingly resilient. They can be strongly exhorted without taking offense. In a way, they consider themselves "fair game" when they listen to a sermon. After all, they say, "That is what we pay the pastor to do; tell us the truth." That is why, in response to a real "pin their ears to the wall" message, you commonly hear, "Thank you, pastor, we really needed to hear that." Scripture tells us to "let it rip." Don't shrink back; tell the truth in love (Jer. 1:5–8; 2 Tim. 2:21–24, 4:2–4). This does not mean the preacher has permission to take out his anxieties and neuroses on the people. The speaker must search his soul, to make sure his motives are pure and that he is distinguishing between personal agenda and clear scriptural truth. On the one hand, no pastor should step away from sermons on adultery, fornication, lying, and gossip, but every pastor should think long and hard before saying political candidates are God's choice because they agree with the pastor on a particular moral issue.

High commitment is to be preached as the norm to all believers, even though it may be practiced by but a few. No spiritual leader is called to make people feel better about their disobedience.

Don't Draw a Line in the Sand

Drawing lines in the sand is hazardous to a church's health, so make sure you don't do it. When it does work, the victory is won under pressure and is usually short-lived. However, if church members don't step across the line, you're out of bullets. "Cross this line or else" is a good way to destroy your motivational credibility. What does a leader do after it doesn't work?

This is particularly true when the leader draws a scripturally "fuzzy" line. It could happen in a moment of anger; it could be asking for a vote of confidence; it could have a connection with the leader's need to succeed. Usually the line is linked to "Do this or I quit." Whether it be the pastor or a lay leader speaking, it's a losing strategy. It polarizes the congregation around issues that are often not central. In some cases a line must be drawn, but let the Scripture be so crystal clear that it depersonalizes the choice. Let God be the one drawing the line; he is uniquely equipped for the task. Just make sure God said it!

There is a better, practical way to get people to the right destination: Leadership can help the congregation actualize the community standards or goals. First the leadership should prayerfully agree on the community standards; then the pastor should present them from the pulpit. Those expectations must meet the criteria of clearly revealed scriptural teaching. Then we face the real challenge: leading people where we believe God has told us to go. If the first step to establishment of a high-commitment environment is the pastor defining normal from the pulpit, then the link to complete credibility is consistent practice of those norms.

Practice, Practice, Practice

The practice of high commitment on the part of leadership is the backbone of the high-commitment environment. If the practices of the church leadership do not support the teaching, the standards will be ignored, and the congregation's commitment will be low.

However, it is not easy or natural for leaders to maintain high standards, because it requires difficult decisions. Part of that difficulty is allowing people to eliminate themselves from leadership; a second component is for leadership not to allow people to ascend to influence without submission to the high-commitment standards. No one really knows or believes what that rhetoric looks like in practice until the standards are enforced and people do not operate on a business-as-usual basis.

Jesus demonstrated the power and the price of not retreating from the value of high commitment. He wept over an unresponsive Jerusalem, but he didn't allow his emotions to cloud his judgment. Once people heard the message, he invited them to follow. If they chose not to, he didn't lower the requirements. It is not loving to mislead your followers into the false belief that superficial spirituality will be rewarded by God. Several months after Jesus had chosen the twelve to "be with him" (Mark 3:14) and only a few months before the cross, there was a confrontation at Capernaum concerning commitment.

Confronted by the religious establishment's representatives, Jesus told them he was the "bread of life" and "no one can come to me unless the Father . . . draws him, and I will raise him up at the last day" (John 6:44, 48). Of course, these comments were blasphemous to the Jewish leaders, and no one was surprised by their displeasure. But then Jesus told them, "I tell you the truth, unless you eat the flesh of the Son of Man and drink his blood, you have no life in you. Whoever eats my flesh and drinks my blood has eternal life, and I will raise him up at the last day. For my flesh is real food and my blood is real drink. Whoever eats my flesh and drinks my blood remains in me, and I in him" (John 6:53–56). The Pharisees were appalled, and the disciples were scared. Jesus was locked in a conflict where the stakes were high. His followers were disoriented, even shocked.

It is expected that the unbelieving world, both religious and secular, will oppose the clear, unyielding Christian message. By *unyielding*, I refer to the total package, including Jesus being the only way to God and eternal punishment in a real place called hell. The message scandalizes the syncretistic world, and many Christians wilt in the heat of its demands. Such claims of absolute truth and the knowledge of the narrow way prescribed by Jesus offend the unregenerate mind. The non-Christian mind longs for an easy answer that allows plenty of moral "wiggle" room. Secular society's greatest sin is intolerance; the Christian's greatest sin is insubordination. That is why one of the last things Jesus told his followers was that the world would reject the message and hate the messengers (John 15:18–21; 16:33).

CHRISTIANS WHO DON'T LIKE CHRISTIAN TRUTH

Revulsion in the face of Christian truth is not the exclusive right of unbelievers. Many evangelicals can't stomach some of Jesus' teachings either. Even some of those following Jesus in his day decided that the requirements were unrealistic. "On hearing it, many of his disciples said, 'This is a hard teaching. Who can accept it?'" (John 6:60). Jesus' response was not to do the contemporary theological backstroke, lowering the heat in order to keep his followers in tow. He told them what he taught was truth and that their response might be an evidence that they really didn't believe. Although they had gotten captured by the excitement, when things got difficult, they were really not with him.

The sad result was the departure of many of his followers. It comes as somewhat of a surprise that Jesus didn't say, "If you change your mind, come on back." Jesus didn't run after those who rejected his teaching. A bigger surprise was his immediate comment to the twelve. He didn't say, "Whew! I'm sure glad you guys are sticking with me. Without you, there would be no way to finish the task, and I would need to start over." Instead he demonstrated the importance of truth over personnel by saying, "You do not want to leave too, do you?" (v. 67). This was their best chance to opt out of what they knew would be a risky future.

Say what you will about the foibles of this suspect band of disciples, but at least say, in most cases, they hung in there and stayed committed. The clear lesson is that the committed stay, and they stay because they have tasted the reality of God. Anything less is not worth living for. "Simon Peter answered him. 'Lord, to whom shall we go? You have the words of eternal life. We believe and know that you are the Holy One of God'" (v. 68). True believers are committed.

This conflict teaches us that many who say, "I am a Christian," are exposed for what they really are when the chips are down. Even in light of all our good theological systems, I am afraid that much the same thing happens today when church members are confronted with the full range of Jesus' demands on their lives.

THE MULTILEVEL COMMITTED SOCIETY

A variety of worldviews, theological understandings, and personal agendas that conflict with the high-commitment ethos populate the church. The key to making high commitment normal is refusal to reward the abnormal. Honoring those progressing in commitment and allowing those not ready for commitment to retreat with dignity will effectively accomplish this goal. The institution of the church allows the not-ready person to retreat into his or her own level of ministry. People can be nurtured, even though they are not doing well spiritually. A church can maintain high standards and at the same time can offer an affirming atmosphere. Make a clear distinction between behavior and a person's intrinsic value to God; a clear difference exists between requirements for leadership and acceptance into the family of God.

The pastor speaks from the pulpit and sets the agenda and standards. He preaches high commitment and does not back off on what it means to be a good and mature follower of Jesus. At the same time, various dignified retreats are available to the not quite ready.

People are not ready for a variety of reasons; they could be seekers or believers going through a time of testing. They could be engaged in a hidden, destructive lifestyle that has not surfaced. Additional obstacles include obsession with work, recreation, or accumulation of material goods, which all can cause a person to stagnate or lose ground. Finally there are those who have burned out or rusted out through years of "church work" and lost sight of the "work of the church"; often these people think they have done their thing for God, so now let someone else try these new ideas. This group may comprise nearly half or more of many congregations, and they can be encouraged to retreat to good and helpful ministries that do not require high commitment. Some of these important ministries are the choir, adult Sunday school, or other fellowship groups. Even many boards or committees do not threaten to require an advanced state of spiritual development. Many small groups are also wonderful resting places.

That is why the high-commitment society is composed of leaders along with a few others who are the walking and talking illustration of the society's values. The majority, however, follow their leaders at a safe distance, some in awe, some in defeat, but all understanding that the society honors high commitment and refuses to reward the lack of it. All that is required to identify the church as a high-commitment society is the commitment of the leadership to scriptural standards in both dogma and personal practice. There is no need to require that all members must be highly committed, any more than every person in a church needs to give money for it to be considered a good giving church.

Therefore, two things are required to establish the high-commitment environment: It must be proclaimed from the pulpit, and the reward structure of the church must be consistent with the preaching.

LEADERS MUST SCORE A BEHAVIORAL "DIRECT HIT"

After laying the scriptural foundation, nothing is more crucial to success than the behavior of the corporate leadership. The actions and choices made by the leadership should score a "direct hit" on the church's mission statement. If the mission is to make disciples who glorify God and reproduce, starting in their own Jerusalem, then the leaders must be making disciples where they live, work, and play.

First, leaders must be trained before they become candidates to lead. The entire church training program should facilitate the development and selection of this kind of person. There is nothing more convincing than a church proclaiming, "Our purpose is to make disciples," and for the pastor to point to a leader and say, "This is what we mean. This person has those characteristics."

Step 2: Keep the Mission in Front of Them

Once the mission is clearly presented verbally and is supported by the community ethos, the challenge is to fight off spiritual amnesia. A most common corporate pathology is losing sight of the goal, especially concerning intangible things. Motor car company workers have little trouble recalling that it is making automobiles. The church, however, easily forgets that it is making disciples. Churches get sidetracked onto many good projects that are part of the task, but in changing their focus, they lose sight of the larger issues. That is why a church can hold numerous Bible studies, conduct youth work, care for the helpless and sick, and support world missions, but not reach anyone new for Christ. Many a church is composed of well-meaning Christians untrained in ministry skills and uncoached in their reason for existence. It is quite common for no one in the church membership to be able to state the church's objective, the criteria for becoming a leader, or how one makes intentional spiritual progress in the church. This lack of focus leads to mediocrity of ministry and disunity.

When submission to the larger purpose is gone, individual agendas take the church hostage. How many hours have been lost, how many pastors have resigned, how many opportunities have been lost when the church finds itself locked in an intramural battle? Many of these diversions and distractions can be avoided by keeping the mission front and center.

The Mission Comes First

Jesus put it plainly, "If anyone would come after me, he must deny himself and take up his cross daily and follow me. . . . What good is it for a man to gain the whole world, and yet lose or forfeit his very self?" (Luke 9:23–25).

When the mission comes first, then God comes first. When God comes first, his promises work. "But whoever loses his life for me will save it" (Luke 9:24). The greatest profit for any individual is to relinquish control of his or her own personal agenda and serve the greater cause. This leads to finding life, and that means finding satisfaction, self-respect, and an inner joy that money can't buy.

Contrary to popular culture's value of self as first, the Christian leader is most loving when he calls the church to sacrifice. It is not compassionate to allow the people of God to wallow in the opulence of their own self-centered agendas. Catering to carnal desire leads to a decay of character and finally to a spiritual death. If we sow to the flesh, from the flesh we will reap (Gal. 6:6–9). Spiritual leaders should be fanatical about priority of the mission.

Keep the vision before people by weaving it into sermons as illustrative windows, in order to help the congregation refocus. The vision must be supported by many decisions made by leadership and voiced by their representatives whenever the goals and values are challenged. Much erosion of vision takes place in the ministry trenches. It might be that small-group leader who is asked to compromise on requirements for group membership. It might be allowing a person who has not earned the right to advance in ministry leadership and influence. Compromise dressed as compassion, flexibility, and relevancy often becomes an enemy of ministry integrity. The competing agendas of church members tend to fuzz the focus, and without realizing it, a ministry can lose its cutting edge.

Part of leadership training is to insist on the urgency and importance of corporate goals. The leadership, both elected and appointed, both board members and small-group leaders, must believe that there is no more important work.

It is more important than global warming, rebuilding Eastern Europe, and solving the Mideast conflict. This vision gives people a sense of importance, and they feel that they are part of a life-changing movement. Your goal is that when people think of the church they think of the mission. As Jonathan Edwards prayed, "Oh God, stamp eternity on my eyeballs." Anytime the eyes are open, the church's mission is perpetually in the foreground. This vivid image communicates that all of life is seen through the lens of eternity and God's values. The desired image, of course, disappears if not regularly imprinted through verbal and behavioral reinforcement.

One afternoon while in a department store I walked into the jewelry section and was startled by what I saw. An elderly man stood with his unconscious wife stretched out on the floor in front of him. He was mumbling something like, "I knew we did too much. We were on our feet too long." Obviously, he was entering a mild state of shock. I rushed over and arrived simultaneously with a gaggle of department store personnel. The delegation was armed with chairs, wet cloths, a first aid kit, and no doubt a legal document or two to be signed. In the midst of the whirling around her, the woman began to regain consciousness. We helped her onto a chair. Someone asked if she needed water, another asked how she was. An employee questioned, "Do you want anything?" Without any hesitation, the half-awake woman pointed to the jewelry counter. "Yes, I want that silver bracelet." We all burst out laughing, and I thought, *There is a woman who never lost sight of her mission.*

The enemy throws many obstacles in the path of obedience, but if the mission is regularly woven into the church's community life, it will be remembered just as clearly as the woman in the department store remembered her mission.

Step 3: Establish Faithfulness

Faithfulness is the rite of passage to any meaningful Christian experience. Various clubs and organizations have their entry-level traditions that make it possible for new members to adhere and to advance. The Israeli Army requires all soldiers to run up the historic Masada at night, with a torch in hand. They stand in the darkness above the Dead Sea and sing their national anthem. Athletic teams engage in mild forms of hazing to initiate their rookies. There always seems to be some hurdle for the new member to clear. You will be glad to know there is no "evangelical hazing"; there is, however, a basic entry-level requirement. The gross failure of Christian leaders to maintain this standard has done great damage to the cause of Christ.

Paul taught and practiced this rite of passage. "Now it is required that those who have been given a trust must prove faithful" (1 Cor. 4:2). After providing Timothy with a long list of character qualities important to leadership, Paul mentions, "They must first be tested; and then if there is nothing against them, let them serve as deacons" (1 Tim. 3:10). Not only did Paul teach that faithfulness was basic entry-level commitment, he cautioned against giving the unfaithful anything valuable. "And the things you have heard me say in the presence of many witnesses entrust to reliable men who will also be qualified to teach others" (2 Tim. 2:2). The plain and simple theme is that proving oneself faithful is a prelude to responsibility. If they don't have to earn it, leaders won't appreciate and won't respect it.

A Little Leads to a Lot

Jesus introduced a method one can use to build commitment and eliminate those committed to not being faithful. In the context of money, Jesus stated, "No servant can serve two masters. Either he will hate the one and love the other, or he will be devoted to the one and despise the other. You cannot serve both God and Money" (Luke 16:13). He preceded this absolute and riveting truth with the passageway to such commitment. "Whoever can be trusted with very little can also be trusted with much, and whoever is dishonest with very little will also be dishonest with much. So if you have not been trustworthy in handling worldly wealth, who will trust you with true riches" (Luke 16:10–11).

The overall principle is that a person must establish that he is at least committed enough to carry out basic assignments and complete them as assigned and on time. Whatever a person demonstrates on a small level is the best predictor for the future. If a person does not prove faithful on this level, he does not proceed to the next level. Paul called Christian responsibility a trust (1 Cor. 4:2), a service (1 Tim. 3:10), and "the things you have heard me say" (2 Tim. 2:2). Jesus referred to the responsibility as "true riches" (Luke 16:11). Any Christian leader can clearly recognize that a person's faithfulness is demonstrated in action, and it becomes the basic entry-level requirement for any future leader.

Do Not Proceed without It

Violation of this simple concept has stocked evangelical churches with the moderately committed, unproven, and unfaithful leaders. It's like building a house on a foundation of cottage cheese. The sad result is that a low-commitment level seems normal, and then it becomes acceptable for leaders to treat God's work like a service organization. In fact they get the attitude that the church is lucky to get the time it does. So projects are done poorly, turned in late, and generally are underfunded. Leaders miss important meetings because unexpected relatives turn up from out of town. Didn't Jesus say something about priorities along these lines? (Luke 14:25–35). People think that staying late at work or at Uncle Frank's retirement party are acceptable reasons to be unfaithful, because leaders have accepted such substandard behavior, and there are no negative consequences. If we want highly committed leaders who do good work, then we weed out the unfaithful via the process taught and modeled by Christ.

There is no expectation of perfection in what is being taught, but we are looking for a pattern of behavior establishing faithfulness in people. Over time I have always been able to discern whether a person is really sincere in his or her attempts to be faithful or is using the standard excuses. If a person is progressing in a positive direction, then weaknesses can be specifically addressed while in motion. Many leaders face the challenge of establishing a churchwide system that reinforces and rewards faithfulness and provides growers with a "fast track" on which to run.

Look Out for These Types

DR. DONALD D. DIVINITY PH.D. BVD.

You're lucky to have him in your congregation; he didn't tell you that, but the look on his face did. He listens to your sermons and periodically nods approval, as if to say, "Not quite right, but not bad." There are a few times when that little smirk appears on his face as it changes colors, and you know that you just mispronounced a Greek word or the name of an Assyrian king or some ancient biblical city. Afterward he launches a benign salvo like, "Thank you for your faithfulness to the Word, pastor." His mother taught him to always find something positive to say. He offers to fill the pulpit, teach an adult Bible class, or to check your sermon accuracy as a service to your ministry.

As he becomes known, members of the congregation approach you with the idea that you give the good doctor a major responsibility, due his evangelical stature. When this happens to you (and it usually does), don't fall into the trap of making an exception to your commitment for all leaders to prove themselves faithful. The good professor may have proven himself smart, but the jury is still out on faithful. Being a faithful Christian and a leader in theology is not the same thing as being proven faithful in ministry in the local church. The ability to understand and communicate material is not the same thing as understanding and communicating with people with a purpose of growth and development. Some very smart theologians are also competent in leadership, but don't confuse knowledge with know-how and leadership or faithfulness.

MR. MADE DE MONEE

The world scrapes and grovels in the presence of large sums of money. Many a Christian leader has lost his dignity in an attempt to fund the Lord's work. In the words of the songwriter, "A little bit of drool let me down." We have given the wealthy prominence and position that far exceed any spiritual qualifications. They sit on boards of churches, universities, and mission organizations for only one reason. Jesus told us this worship of money was the antithesis of service to God.

Before you protest, it should be said there are many happy exceptions to this rule. But it is still the rule that many ministries are held hostage to some eccentric person of means who is accustomed to using money as a hammer for getting his or her way. What is so dangerous is that often that way is the way of the world and a violation of Scripture.

The most egregious manifestation is in the older, wealthy power broker, who exhibits a condescending attitude toward his younger, local church pastor. Generally early, sometimes in the first week of the pastor's work, an invitation is extended to a harmless lunch or dinner at the impressive home of the wealthy member. During the course of the meal, the wealthy member tries to establish several boundaries and communicate the "pecking order." "I have a lot of influence around here, and if you want to succeed, you will need both my blessing and my money" is the message. Though this may not ever be voiced by the person, many willing surrogates volunteer these obvious truths.

Money may also be used to control those special projects that are vital to the church. A humble wealthy person would simply respond to the need as it is made to the church populace. Some wealthy persons, however, expect a private and personal appeal from the pastor before they go on record as having done this for the church.

Finally the most repugnant form of control is deliberate withholding of funds until a project is done the way the person of wealth wants it. Sometimes the member will grandstand by personally funding a new staff position or project. This gives one person undue influence and control of the church.

Early in the life of our church plant we had a $2,000-a-month budget. A person of means who volunteered to be church administrator gave 50 percent of that figure. (One does wonder about the need for a church administrator in a church of 100, but he had the degree mounted on an attractive plaque, and he wanted to use it and have others see it prominently hung above the nice desk he had personally purchased.)

After a while, he and his wife determined that they didn't care for the music in our worship services and demanded that we change. The benefit to us would be their donation of a new and expensive organ. He sat me down and told me that he gave 50 percent of our budget and wondered how we might make it without his money. I told him thanks for the offer of the organ, but we didn't need one, and our church was not for sale. The couple left the church and took their plaques, desks, and money with them. They also took their negative spirit and controlling attitude.

How did we make it without 50 percent of our income? We hardly noticed. God simply provided. Remember, God is our source, no single person or group of persons. People who try to grab power in the church via money make me sick, and they make God sick too.

If a wealthy person in your church employs any of these tactics, I would advise you not to fall for it. Make it clear to the entire congregation that you don't believe in investing; you believe in giving with no strings attached. Let it be clear that the church is not for sale at any price. You are not willing to threaten the integrity of your mission or decision-making process through appointed leaders by allowing money to buy decisions or votes. You may make an enemy, but you will gain the respect of God and most of the congregation. It may be rough sailing for a while, but in the long run the rewards are great for not allowing money to control your work, particularly in the selection of leaders. Remember, the problem in context is breaking entry-level requirements to establish faithfulness because of other, less important, qualifications.

Systems Approach

The systems approach to developing people is the way of Jesus. It is loving, responsible, and biblical.

Remove from your mind, if you will, the stereotypical systems analyst. He has on a short-sleeve white shirt with a bad tie and a pocket protector. His polyester slacks are tight and shiny, and his wing tips need polish. He plays by the numbers and is convinced that numbers don't lie (what he doesn't know is neither do they tell a story).

A system doesn't need to be unfeeling, rigid, and out of touch with humanity. Jesus used a simple systems approach to teach his followers and sort out the most committed from the less committed.[1] A good system allows seekers to enter easily, but requires greater and greater commitment to advance. As people advance they by necessity learn more and acquire greater skill. They grow in their understanding of who they are and how they can best contribute to the cause of Christ. They will also get to know God better and develop a more intimate relationship with Christ and fellow Christians. The development of integrity and faithfulness can be built into the system. That way leaders have the luxury of allowing the "cream to rise to the top" and then can focus on those who are developing positive behavioral patterns. Whatever you choose, you cannot allow people to proceed to leadership unless they have earned it objectively and are proven faithful.

Step 4: Help Them over Obedience Barriers

People development begins with general sweeping truths and then gradually becomes more specific as a person makes progress. The largest group, at the top of the funnel, has been exposed to the concepts of high commitment via the creation of a high-commitment environment, and that is supported by keeping the mission front and center. The next step is that many will enter the establishment-of-faithfulness phase. This is generally accomplished through their participation in low-commitment, entry-level small groups and special projects. Commonly the eager easily establish themselves as faithful in the little things. It must be remembered, however, that this happens much more easily when the entire community ethos rewards faithfulness and punishes the lack of it by limiting advancement. If the environment doesn't reinforce community standards, the establishment of faithfulness as normal will be very difficult.

The Barriers

I have often stated that without accountability you can't make disciples. Accountability is helping others keep their commitments to God. There are no exceptions to the rule that we need others' help in making our spiritual journey as productive as possible. If people could read the Bible or hear a message and then go out and live the Christian life without encouragement, correction, or discipline, we would need only Bibles, but not churches. Any casual observer of human behavior knows how naive such a belief actually is. Few among us—there may be none—haven't needed someone to come along and help us over an obedience barrier (or two or three hundred) during our lives. So many never grow beyond the formative stages, because the deeper, more troubling issues never surface in a superficial evangelical environment. Because there is very little serious discipling going on that challenges people to root out emotional and spiritual pathology, most carry the pathologies into leadership and, just as tragically, into family life.

When pastors and church leaders refuse to break down their congregation into intentional small communities that help people deal with their real problems, they are refusing to develop people. For years many have simply asked people to come hear them preach in multiple services, give money, and serve on committees. This grievous error has led to a well-informed church populated by the guilt ridden, the jaded, or the misled, all experts on what they are not experiencing. You can't get at people by simply talking to them or working on ministry projects. When the spiritual barriers are not dealt with, these pathologies manifest themselves in unfinished projects, hurt feelings, grabbing for power, and emotional breakdown.

I often think of the church as people standing in a large field, all trying to move in the same direction. At one end of the field is the goal, Christlikeness. People are standing at various stages of the journey: Some have made good progress, others very little, most are somewhere in the middle. Most are not moving because they all stand in front of a very high barrier that they can't seem to get over on their own. This barrier is personal and different for each individual. These are obedience barriers, the sins or difficulties that continue to dominate their lives. All of us have the besetting sins, the chronic sins that are our weaknesses. It seems as if every time we start making good progress, we get blocked by our chronic sin. At this point, if our church is rightly configured, someone will be aware of our problem and will be ready to throw us a rope to help us scale the barrier and move on.

Obedience barriers are varied and almost always camouflaged. One leader told me he was too busy to become an elder. He claimed he was overworked and overcommitted and that the church had required too much of him in a leadership role. He didn't mention the money and time he spent on golf, the many sporting events he attended, or the various trips and vacations he took. All he knew was that he was out of time and money. There was no way to immediately challenge everything he said, but I knew the issues were deeper. A few weeks later he approached me to tell me of his ongoing affair with a woman at work; the guilt and emotional turmoil at home made it impossible for him to lead.

If we had known of his marital issues and his struggle in the workplace, someone could have helped him over that obedience barrier. But for this to happen the Christian needs to grant those around him two things, proximity and permission. Proximity means regular access to him, so they can get to know him well and establish trust. Permission means that once trust is developed, he grants permission for someone to enter his life and to talk about the real issues.

"Pastor, I'm Burned Out"

Quite often active church members will use the term *burnout* to describe why they cannot complete tasks or maintain commitments. Almost always they tend to blame the church for the problem. This is quite common, especially when the real problem is hidden and they want to divert attention away from personal responsibility, to maintain some dignity. A would-be leader might challenge a method of training, when the real problem is fear. A man might choose not to submit to training "because it's too controlling," when the real issue is pride. A woman may decide she cannot lead a group because she "doesn't have the time," when the real culprit is laziness. The difference between much of what happens in churches today and what I advocate is that I suggest we get at the real problem, the chronic sin, the barrier to obedience, and win over it. When you do confront the real problem, you will learn a great deal about the person, and this can predict his or her spiritual future.

HOW DO YOU TAKE CORRECTION?

"Whoever corrects a mocker invites insult; whoever rebukes a wicked man incurs abuse. Do not rebuke a mocker or he will hate you; rebuke a wise man and he will love you. Instruct a wise man and he will be wiser still; teach a righteous man and he will add to his learning" (Prov. 9:7–9).

How a person reacts to correction is a predictor of his or her spiritual future. No one enjoys being corrected, but having the humility to receive it and the wisdom to learn from it is essential to spiritual growth. The corrective action makes life better, while it roots pride, a roadblock to Christlikeness, out of our lives. A person who does not accept correction should not be a leader; he or she will not even be a mature Christian. There are far too many untamed egos in Christian leadership. The pollution of the cultural understanding of leadership has spilled over into the Christian community. Canards such as "Never admit you're wrong or apologize," "Never let them see you sweat," "Don't show signs of weakness," and "Make sure you have all the markings of power (such as the right car,

car phone, and suit of clothes to give you that critical edge)" have trickled into the Christian mainstream but they have not changed Christian truth. Being open to correction and to the opinions of others is a sign of strength.

The Support Structure

Again the advantage of the systems approach is to create a progression of small groups or communities built on proximity and permission. These groups provide the most powerful accountability (namely love and support) as members progress and the challenges become greater. This structure helps people over obedience barriers and creates good habits that make growth possible. Such disciplines include meaningful interaction with the Scriptures, learning to pray, and appreciating the power of community and the joy and responsibility of outreach. These are the heart of Christian faith and must be mastered in order to reach spiritual maturity and purposeful living.

Those who have decided to move toward high commitment and have entered your support structure that establishes faithfulness and challenges them to get over obedience barriers, become your fishing pool for apprenticeship. The next logical step in the development of commitment is to give them an important assignment. When they enter apprenticeship, they are formally moving toward leadership. Without some system to both build and eliminate, you will have an empty pool and no possibility of finding well-trained, proven personnel for the next level. You can always find a warm body and willing spirit, but why accept mediocrity?

Step 5: Give Them Responsibility

An apprenticeship is a time of learning a craft or set of skills, while bound to a mentor. It implies a desire on the part of the apprentice to learn and a belief on the part of the mentor that the apprentice can learn. The two parties have made an agreement: The mentor will teach, and the apprentice will work alongside. There is a special bond, as the apprentice has committed to submit to the authority and leadership of the teacher. It also means that the apprentice has met preliminary qualifications in order to be chosen for the position.

Jesus modeled the results of apprenticeship when he sent out the twelve on their first major mission without his physical presence. In the tenth chapter of his Gospel, Matthew recorded Jesus' set of instructions. Jesus told them where to go, what to say, when to leave, even what they should take in their suitcases. They went out and experienced mission under tight guidelines, and then they returned to debrief with their teacher.

If our delegation is done well, we will do it the same way Jesus did: We'll be clear, detailed, and we'll keep it simple.

Develop a Farm System

Another argument for the creation of effective disciple-making systems that include apprenticeship is that they aid in the accurate selection of future leaders. How many times have older leaders lamented the lack of newer leaders. There are two reasons for the lament: Usually the lamenters are not trainers, and the leadership they are modeling is so unattractive that the spiritual young lions don't aspire to the bureaucratic leadership model. The effective disciple-making system creates a steady flow of candidates for higher commitment because they have established themselves in the structure. Since proximity and permission have been largely established, group leaders can make the best selection of the next generation. I speak here of a spiritual generation rather than a chronological one. In other words, "the cream rises to the top." But existing leaders need to be trained in what to look for and must take steps to recruit, when appropriate.

Training provides you with a farm system of future leaders who are well trained and have some experience. In both *The Disciple-Making Pastor* and *The Disciple-Making Church* I have written in detail concerning the importance of a leadership community. For present purposes I want to speak only of the importance of a separate environment for leaders and their apprentices. First, a would-be leader should be tested in the requirements of leadership (1 Tim. 3:10). The heart of training is showing the apprentice what to do and then doing with the apprentice what he is going to do with others. Additionally it means to let him do it under the tutelage of the mentor. The basic rite of passage is the establishment of faithfulness; the next step is entry into the leadership fraternity. Several characteristics mark this special environment.

Desire

No one who does not aspire to lead should be in a leadership environment. Eager spirits are required, and they have already demonstrated the interest, or they would not have been chosen by their group leaders or persons working close enough to have observed their lives and ministries. That decision is confirmed by the recognized head of the ministry (the pastor or staff member or a lay leader who has the authority).

The fastest way to destroy the leadership community is to allow the wrong people to join. The only agenda is that would-be leaders must give it their all, submit to their teachers, and learn to be the leaders God has called them to be. Scripture counsels us to count the cost before we commit to build a tower. Spiritual leaders are building more than a tower; they are building the kingdom of God.

Understanding Ministry

The most important characteristic of a leader is what he thinks. As an apprentice, he must review his worldview and how he relates to those around him. He must understand what his life means in the larger drama of God's redemptive plan. What role does the church play in that drama, and how does he personally fit? This is the reason that once a person becomes an apprentice, the mentor must immediately begin to upgrade his biblical/philosophical understanding of the church and more specifically the local church. The apprentice must be trained to keep the larger good of the church in mind. Nonleaders, young leaders, and untrained leaders tend to think in small "sound bites." They develop an anecdotal theology from stories and experiences. It worked in Fred's life; then it should for others as well. While experience is crucial to a well-rounded theology, it cannot serve as the foundation. Building an anecdotal theology will bring disaster, for it will be too subjective to stand against the real issues of life. For this reason all apprentices spend the first year in a special study program that helps them understand and write a personal and corporate philosophy of ministry. They are working on other on-the-job projects as well, but this self-study is a nonnegotiable.

THE COVENANT

"You're in the big leagues now," we tell the apprentices. "You have counted the cost, and it will be higher than ever before. The stakes are high, and we plan to entrust you with 'true riches'—the care and development of God's children. You must work hard to be the very best leaders you can be. Anything less is sin." For that reason we issue to them a covenant that includes all the requirements and expectations. It includes such things as time commitment (both in weeks and in years); it also lists books to read and projects to complete. The most important aspect is their submission to the authority of both the community itself and their mentor. It makes clear that we love them so much that we are going to help them keep their commitment to God. Not everyone makes it through the training: Some drop out;

some are asked to leave. The covenant mentions all the benefits that will result when apprentices complete their apprenticeships. If they do well, the next step will be their opportunity to have a group or ministry of their very own.

I am not including an example of our covenant in the book for fear you will copy and use it. It's not that I worry about copyright, but I believe you should develop your own.

Playing with a Bad Referee

In my final high school basketball game in the Indiana State Basketball Tournament, we were matched against a team we had defeated a week earlier. The game was interesting, and after exchanging leads during the first thirty minutes, the final two minutes found us tied.

The opposition was bringing the ball down the floor, and one of our guards stole the ball and was breaking away for an uncontested basket that would have put us ahead. He was already several steps down the floor when the official blew his whistle (this is referred to as a "late call").

Our player was very angry, and our coach was livid. Our player went up to the official and asked, "What did I do?"

The official called a technical foul, which took away our basket and our lead and gave the other team both a foul shot and the ball. This turned the game significantly in the opponent's favor, and they won the game. When questioned by our coach concerning the technical, the official claimed "the young man cussed me." One thing we know for sure: Our player did not curse or use any profanity.

That night our guard (now my friend) learned that life is not fair. The adult official lied to our coach in order to save his own hide.

That is the plight of playing with a bad referee. Once the game begins, you can protest, scream, and do many other things, but you can't get rid of that official. He has been chosen, and you have to make the best of it.

Working with untrained leaders is like playing with a bad referee. You're stuck with them for a while, and you cannot do a great deal about it. You get poor performance, and you get it again and again until the bad leader moves, quits, dies, or his term runs out. That's no way to run a church. Leadership training is too important not to be taken seriously.

Whatever you do, make training relevant with on-the-job experience. Cognitive training must be joined with a work assignment. This way apprentices will have a built-in "felt need" to learn, and they will learn faster and enjoy it more. To simply stick future leaders in a classroom and teach abstracts will do serious harm in the long run. Everyone thinks training should be done the way they were trained, but being told what to do is only the beginning of the process. Let us not perpetuate a nontraining model as training. Make sure there is a critical balance between telling people what to do and offering practical opportunities.

Step 6: Give Them Leadership

In 1860 the following ad appeared in a San Francisco newspaper on behalf of the Pony Express. "Wanted: young, skinny, wiry fellows, not over 18, must be expert riders willing to risk daily: Orphans Preferred." The obvious message is that the faint of heart need not apply. The church must give a similar warning to those who would lead. You do not need the fainthearted in your leadership group. When you challenge apprentices to take part in full leadership, also require a recommitment. Before you commission leaders and expand their ministry influence, review where they are.

It was my custom to review several biblical passages concerning leadership with new leaders. The most prominent was 1 Timothy 3:1: "Here is a trustworthy saying: If anyone sets his heart on being an overseer, he desires a noble task."

People who commit to lead must do it because their hearts are set on it; they desire to do the task. They do not desire the influence, the power, or the prestige; it's the ministry they long for. They need to be reminded that it will stretch them; it will make them glad, sad, and sometimes so frustrated they will want to scream. Like the Pony Express ad, the faint of heart or the weak of will need not proceed. This major checkpoint is to be taken seriously before an apprentice goes on to greater influence and responsibility.

The first shock to a new leader is that he no longer has a mentor to turn to in a meeting. No other person there has the authority he possesses to make decisions. It has become his responsibility, and it often sends chills up and down his spine. (Sometimes he will be tempted to check to see if his spine is still intact.) Many a person who has been promoted to the position of top leader in an organization has suddenly been consumed by fear as the full weight of this new responsibility comes to bear. It happens to the Sunday school teacher and the small-group leader as well. When Jesus called the twelve to be with him in order to send them out to preach, reality didn't hit until he had ascended and they were waiting for something to happen. It's much like the time when driver's education is over: There is no longer an experienced driver sitting next to you, with a separate brake that can save all passengers from disaster. You're now behind the wheel alone; that is why the insurance is so high.

Mistakes Leaders Make

How often I sought and gained agreement from small-group leaders, only to have them collapse in the face of opposition. When I quizzed them as to why they "folded in the clutch," the usual defense was "I didn't really understand or believe in that concept." For pastors this is one of those "I would like to tear my hair out, scream from a rooftop, or drive into the sunset and not come back" moments.

As I gained experience in training leaders, I came to understand the above process as normal. An untested faith is worth very little; so are untested beliefs. Over the years I have faithfully laid before new leaders the principles that work best and have stood the test of time. They then proceed to disregard some of them and pollute almost all of them. They do the right things but often do not do them right. They might engage in the right activities but fail to do them in the proper sequence, thus reducing their effectiveness.

AVOIDING REALITY

One leader, under the leadership of the Holy Spirit (at least he said so), decided to give evangelism a new name. His group would call it love. Who could object to that? you might ask. I did, and I had a good reason: He changed the name because his group was afraid to do evangelism. He renamed it so they wouldn't have to do it. Each group was required to do evangelistic outreach; the idea was to pray for and then invite non-Christian friends to a social event. At that event someone would give a testimony, or the Christian message would be presented. Group members were trained then to share Christ and even how to do basic follow-up.

I attended this very loving group's first "love in." Not one couple brought a guest; some of the group members were even missing.

This remains one of the more creative attempts by a new leader to avoid the realities of human nature. People naturally take the road most traveled, the path of least resistance. He failed the test, but once he did, he was open to be taught. I am happy to say he corrected his error, and the group excelled. They simply needed to acknowledge fear, then allow Christ to help them overcome it. The leader met the challenge by first overcoming his own fear and then leading the group to success.

IGNORING STRUCTURE

Another creative type decided to run his group in reverse. The normal sequence for that kind of group was Bible study for an hour, sharing for twenty minutes, outreach training for twenty minutes, and prayer for twenty minutes. The time frames have some flex built in, but the sequence of events was crucial to the group's goals. This group started with sharing; people would come in with the battle scars and open wounds and the events of the day fresh in their minds. This sharing was considered therapeutic; they called it a "buffer zone," but it nearly destroyed the group. People came in with their anger and frustration and oftentimes a fleshly perspective on themselves and their problems. Most weeks the group would share and pray, and their time was gone.

The purpose of doing Bible study first was to draw God's perspective on all of life, including their felt needs. That gave the group a compass heading for the evening. Also excluded most weeks was the outreach training the group needed to help them extend outside themselves and to give them much needed relief from self-absorption.

When the group started to flounder because it was going nowhere, I was able to move in and make the proper corrections. The group leader gained an appreciation for structure and its importance in developing people.

HANDING OVER AUTHORITY

One of the more difficult tests for a leader is to maintain his standards for group ethos when he is opposed by his or her spouse. There may not be a more severe test for the Christian leader than a lack of support at the most intimate level. One such leader with a great heart and a teachable spirit launched out into the deep with a new group. Within a few weeks it became apparent that his wife was undermining his authority and breaking group morale. When the outreaches were being planned or training was taking place via role playing, she would roll her eyes. She didn't memorize Scripture and often didn't complete her lesson or keep the commitments she had made. The leader had a choice: Maintain group principles in the face of his angry wife or break faith with his commitment and support his wife in her mutiny.

By the time I attended the group, many of the other women had taken up the offense of the wife. I entered the fray in the face of the proverbial warning, "Like one who seizes a dog by the ears is a passerby who meddles in a quarrel not his own" (Prov. 26:17). I was neither a passerby nor a meddler; I was their leader, so I grabbed on and held on. It was a serious mess. The group had to be reorganized, but the leader and his wife were able to continue; he passed the test.

People of Conviction

One of leadership's frustrations, maybe in the top ten, is leaders who, under pressure from others, defer responsibility to the top leader or pastor. I can think of no character trait more needed among leaders than to be people of conviction and to have the courage to maintain those convictions. When a new leader (or any leader, for that matter) melts in the heat of opposition, it is usually because a belief has not yet become a conviction. I point out to leaders the truth "If you falter in times of trouble, how small is your strength!" (Prov. 24:10). A conviction is a bone-deep belief that you are willing to make any sacrifice to maintain. You are willing to lose friends, make enemies, live with family members mad at you, all because it is a guiding principle of life. A belief turns to conviction when you see it work in people's lives, even when there was much opposition to it. This passage from belief to conviction is a journey every great leader makes.

Peter was eager, young, rough, and ready to lead a high-commitment small group. It turned out that he was also the youngest man in his group. Additionally, his group included two hard-charging, highly successful business leaders who were accustomed to being in command. They had made the commitment necessary to become members of the group but they reserved the right to bring their "worldly wisdom" to bear on the group. I knew this would be a severe test for Peter's leadership. Peter was truly a people person, loving, concerned, and one who always had time to listen. His weakness was the desire to be liked more than to be right. He had a commitment to people over programs, which is often a euphemism for passion over principle.

Until a person is challenged and learns to take personal responsibility for principles, he cannot be a useful leader. For Peter, disciple making was a concept, a mind toy, the pastor's program; it was not yet Peter's thing.

I have often said, "This is no hill to die on." Frequently we excuse ourselves from many difficult problems through such a statement. As I grow older, I find very few hills that I would be willing to ascend and die on. But the principles of discipleship form a hill to die on when you are training leaders. If you want to get exercised over something that really matters as it pertains to your church's well-being, this is it.

By reading Peter's weekly report, I could tell that he was losing control of his group's direction. Morale was in jeopardy, because the two self-proclaimed leaders had broken faith by not keeping their commitments, and the group members who *had* kept their commitments were in danger of losing heart. First I had a conversation with Peter as to why he had allowed the slippage to occur. He confessed that while he agreed with the principles behind the group structure, he lacked the experience required to combat what the two stronger men were saying. I attended the group and demonstrated for Peter how to correct the problem. Subsequently Peter became stronger and better; he took ownership of the principles and was able to stand against those who desired to break down the group.

There are two crucial and wonderful moments in training leaders. The first is when you *give* them leadership; the second is when they *take* leadership. The church is populated with far too many to whom leadership has been given and far too few who have taken it. The reason for this defeating trend is the lack of intentionality of existing leaders, who think that good leadership just happens. Disciples are born to be made; leaders are spiritually born and are gifted to lead, but it only happens when that gifting is seen and they are trained. There are more unidentified, untrained, unused leaders in the church than in most other businesses and organizations. Please remember, if a leader in training will not stand strong in the face of opposition in a small-group setting, he will certainly collapse as a top church leader.

Step 7: Keep Stimulating

Leaders never lose their need to be led. The first six principles tell us how to build commitment; the seventh teaches us how to keep leaders committed and growing. Well-trained leaders can easily lose their way. Often people challenge the veracity of my writing and teaching when they hear that a church I pastored experienced difficulty after I left. They say, "If the leaders you trained made mistakes and didn't carry on as usual, doesn't this void your teaching?" My first response is "I suppose you will be asking Jesus the same question." After his perfect example and training, his followers ran away, and others denied they ever knew him. If the training was perfect (and I believe it was), then the problem was not the training. I am not saying that anything I have ever done is perfect; I know for a fact that much of my work is flawed, but it has been more than adequate to prepare leaders to get the job done well. The more important principle and more powerful issue is the humanity of those trained. Just because people abandon principles doesn't mean they don't know them or even deeply hold to them. It means that the flesh can take control of a person at any unguarded moment, and terrible things can happen. Human nature dictates that we never outgrow our need for accountability or the need for further training.

Following Jesus' Example

Jesus fed 5,000 people with very little food. Not long after that he came walking to the disciples on the water. In the context of this act, the disciples still feared for their lives in the storm. They had not transferred their understanding of God's power to feed someone to knowing he could protect in a storm. Later, after feeding the 4,000, Jesus sent the disciples across the sea, and they were in anguish concerning a lack of food. Again they had not made the connection. What makes this example so astonishing is that even when the transition that was required was food to food, they still didn't get it. Are today's followers of Jesus any smarter? Certainly we are no wiser or more intelligent than men who had the good sense to follow Jesus.

Jesus kept the disciples off balance; class was always in session, and the classroom was life itself. Jesus didn't want his followers to get too comfortable. They needed to be on the edge of their collective seats. In fact one of my guiding principles is that when late adapters to new ideas feel comfortable, I am moving too slowly.

At first, it might seem to present-day leaders that we are at a disadvantage in that we cannot duplicate the spectacular events performed by Jesus. If you think of Jesus' miracles, not in terms of power but in terms of lasting results in the lives of the disciples, you'll see that we are not at too great a disadvantage. We cannot read the hearts of men, as Jesus could, but we can read the Bible, in which God has told us everything we need to know in general concerning people's spiritual condition and what their needs happen to be. Think of ways to nurture leaders' spirits, increase their vision, and build their minds. Look for positive ways to challenge them where they must trust God or fail.

Continued Growth

The writer to the Hebrews spoke of this when he encouraged us to think of ways to stimulate one another to love and good deeds (10:24–25). Jade is a beautiful green stone, but the phrase "to become jaded" speaks to the stone's hardness. Avoid seeing leaders hardened by providing the atmosphere of encouragement that brings growth.

After having unidentified, untrained, and therefore, unused leaders, the next greatest leadership problem is the "know it all, see it all, done it all, don't try to teach me anything" attitude. Church leaders (and the entire populace for that matter) seem to reach a certain level of Christian experience and declare it normal and acceptable. There is the unspoken idea that after we learn so much Bible, have so many experiences, have been on a certain number of missions, as Christians we can go into semiretirement. The learning curve was steep, and now we are ready to cruise. Such leaders have fallen for a deception that could have been averted by this counsel: "See to it, brothers, that none of you has a sinful, unbelieving heart that turns away from the living God. But encourage one another daily, as long as it is called Today, so that none of you may be hardened by sin's deceitfulness" (Heb. 3:12–13).

If leaders are not required to stretch and actually lead others into the teeth of the enemy's stronghold, they will become jaded—robots who simply do functions at church.

That means we all need to be encouraged daily, or on a regular basis, to go on and continue the journey that God has planned for us. I have sat in too many meetings with too many elected or appointed leaders who are on autopilot. They have scaled the heights required to attain leadership status, only to celebrate their arrival, like a Mount Everest victor, and then consider the climb complete. Some will not easily give up the spoils of the victor's life and become climbers once again.

Making sure leaders stay in people-to-people ministry is all that is required for continued growth. You might say, "I know that!" Good! So *do* it. The main reason leaders stagnate is that they become administrators and lose touch with people ministry. If you train people in a disciple-making system that rewards growth and achievement and punishes the opposite, you will make many disciples and train good leaders. If you keep your leaders in that system, working with the people, making decisions about life, death, marriages, and people's proper placement in spiritual life, you will never have to worry about stagnation or hardening of your leaders.

9

Three Steps
That Maintain Commitment

If you want to love people, help them keep their commitments to God.

Do you want to make people angry? Then help them keep their commitments to God.

Are you willing to have well-intentioned, spiritually motivated believers become hostile and turn on you? Then help them keep their commitments to God.

Helping people keep their commitments to God can be a leader's greatest challenge. There is nothing Christians want more; there is nothing they will fight more fiercely. Even though they made the commitment, every negative emotion that resides in the darker side of human personality will surface to take its turn to break the commitment. The great anomaly of life is that people will resist what they desperately desire. They will kick, scream, scratch, and drag their heels on the journey to success.

The Israelites desperately wanted to leave Egypt and enter the promised land. But we all find out what they did.

As then, today there is a wide gulf between desire and commitment. This creates a frustration, even self-pity, in the minds of leaders, who feel a lot like Moses, crying out to God:

> Why have you brought this trouble on your servant? What have I done to displease you that you put the burden of these people on me? Did I conceive all these people? Did I give them birth? Why do you tell me to carry them in my arms, as a nurse carries an infant, to the land you promised an oath to their forefathers. Where can I get meat for all these people? They keep wailing to me, 'Give us meat to eat!' I cannot carry all these people by myself; the burden is too heavy for me. If this is how you are going to treat me, put me to death right now.
>
> Numbers 11:11–15

Lead, Don't Lament

This entire concept of helping people keep their commitments to God is charged with emotion, but managing commitment as a corporate leader is essential. Some like to think that people don't need help, that the Holy Spirit will take care of this difficult business of pointing out defects and spurring people on. Others like to point out the abuses of authority that have been documented by ancient and contemporary church history. Leaders have a choice; we can lament the difficulty of leading and managing people or we can dive in headfirst and accept that part of good leadership is requiring accountability. I do know this: *Not to motivate and call for high commitment with the personal commitment to manage and help people keep their commitments is uncaring and an abdication of responsibility.* Leaders cannot make commitments for others, but they can declare the necessity of commitments to normal Christian living and they can show how keeping commitments is crucial to a Christian's sense of joy and success. It is so unloving to just let people meander around without accountability, because they will continue to fail.

Finally they fear commitment because they've never kept one. This has led to many Christians living in defeat, strangers to victory. If you are not willing to be a counter-cultural leader and help people keep the commitments they have made, get out sackcloth and ashes, because in the long run you will simply author your own version of Lamentations.

How does a leader help people keep their commitments to God? There are three major steps:

1. Create the environment.
2. Set the structure.
3. Manage the commitments.

Step 1: Create the Environment

Leaders create environments by words and actions. But those who never create an environment of authority will undercut their own efforts.

Authority

Authority can be viewed as a friend or as a foe. Properly exercised, it is the best friend any Christian can possess (Prov. 3:1–12; Rom. 13:1–7; 1 Peter 2:13–24).

Structure is part of living in relationship with others. Rules and the authority that enforces them make it possible for groups of people to live together in harmony. Life without authority is unthinkable and would be unlivable.

By submitting to spiritual authority in our lives, we protect ourselves from excess discipline, suffering, and anguish. There is enough suffering already for the believer; why not eliminate the unnecessary amount that we bring on ourselves because we are not under the counsel and leadership of others?

Authority is built on the belief that there are rights and wrongs, and scriptural authority is based on the authority given to Jesus (Matt. 28:18–20). People need to be taught that there is a standard set of absolute scriptural rules that make Christlikeness possible. Otherwise they will do whatever seems right to them—and that is commonly called chaos.

Many churches live in what its leaders like to call creative chaos; in reality it's the seedbed for moral relativism in the evangelical church. In such a congregation, Christians begin to create their own versions of truth. They follow the contemporary tolerance that says, "Whatever is right for you in religion, whatever meets your needs, whatever works for you is true for you."

So many Christians want to report directly to Jesus and have no others interfering with their personal understanding of God's plan for their lives. But there is a wide gulf between going directly to the Father in prayer, via Jesus, by means of the Holy Spirit, and working out your salvation. While its proponents are not willing to admit it, this relativistic soup makes Albert Schweitzer the moral equivalent of a Hitler or Stalin. When there are no absolutes or final judge on morality, then everything is morally equal, based on whatever truth grid you have created.

Self-directed spirituality has never been a good idea, and it never will be. Just as moral relativism is in the process of destroying America, it can also destroy a church.

Among evangelicals, relativism manifests itself in a statement such as, "Whatever that text means to you is what it means." It doesn't make any difference if it's not what the author meant or if it's out of context. Under this ethos many live in bondage to a lie, and that lie is a misinterpreted passage or a poor application of a text. This lack of a firm biblical standard also begins to break down the absolutes as they relate to the "big ticket" items like basic morality. And the concept of spiritual authority erodes much faster.

The church must be counter-cultural by proclaiming that the Scriptures are the absolutes and form a foundation for morality, authority, and meaningful interaction. We do this in a culture that has its fist raised, its back bowed, and its chin jutted out.

Most churches start out right: They adopt credal statements; the correct doctrinal proclamations are made from the pulpit; even the constitution makes mention of rights and responsibilities of the membership. Where the credal statements end is where failure begins. The critical nexus is at the point of actual proclamation from the pulpit and formation of a functional environment that supports the credal statements. If the formal doctrinal environment is not reinforced by the functional environment, then absolutes diminish.

It is quite common for a church to have an absolutist credal environment and a relativistic functional environment. In doctrine we declare, "Here we stand"; in functionality we muse, "Whatever seems to work for you." The difference is illustrated by drawing a distinction between church discipline and spiritual disciplines. By constitution a church must act on behalf of the congregational integrity to discipline those who regularly and grossly violate standards of behavior; this represents the credal or constitutional authority. However, while church discipline is vital to the church's integrity, it is no more important than the much less practiced need to hold members accountable for practicing the spiritual disciplines.

Developing a Community Ethos

As always, congregational expectations are best expressed and developed through the teaching ministry. The most powerful venue is the combination of the moral leader, the pastor, communicating from the most strategic place, the pulpit. Teaching sets the expectations and creates the belief that engagement in those activities will be for the benefit of members and the entire community.

The earliest description of such a positive environment is in Acts 2:42–47. The church devoted itself to the activities that created the community ethos. Those activities were prescribed in the "apostles' teaching." It put a premium on sharing life together and sharing meals, which sometimes included Holy Communion.

It is safe to assume the apostles taught that certain activities were crucial to spiritual development. As the community adopted them as normal, important, and essential, there was the happy result described in the remaining verses. There was a sense of wonder, they were giving, they continued to meet, they went to one another's homes, they were engaged in unbridled praise, and they were reaping a rich harvest in that people were entering the kingdom daily.

The leader's assignment is to convince the populace that these expectations are right and good. Additionally, we must reinforce the idea that in our community we will honor and esteem those who practice them. They will be our leaders; they will be vested with authority and be entrusted with our most valuable asset, the care of God's children.

Nearly every church member has made a commitment to God of some importance. Each really does want to please, serve, and obey God. But many do not know how; they are untrained in the basics or they are bound by habitual sin patterns that continue to defeat them.

Good leaders convince people of the tremendous benefit of submission to others in helping them develop. People enter at their own levels, but the big surprise is that the more they grow, the more accountability they need and, most of the time, desire. When they allow others to encourage and mentor them, their freedom increases. Christian freedom is not doing whatever you want, whenever you want; it is, rather, freedom from the bondage of sin. It is the liberty to obey God, to frolic in the power of his Spirit.

Leaders want Christians to rise from the foundation of spiritual authority and accountability to soar to spiritual heights. Accountability and structure have a trapeze effect. Christians do not fly with the greatest of ease, but with the greatest of preparation. As leaders we first inspire others to commitment; then we must set the structure to make it a reality.

Step 2: Set the Structure

Let me say it again: You can't make disciples without accountability, and you cannot have accountability without structure. If a church is going to develop people, then the question the leaders must consider is "what kind of structure?"

The structure needs certain basics—it should have stages or steps that people can proceed through. Each stage should either stretch members spiritually or, more precisely, place them according to gifts or calling.[1] The system should be based on and reward good motivation, such as experiencing more challenge or doing something more relevant to a person's existing need.

As you establish your system, it is important to understand the level at which a person is functioning. I have been learning to play golf, and it has been very challenging. When it comes to golf, I have learned that it's not as important who you play with as where you play. I compete against the course, but I am playing with my golf partners. If I play with very good players, on a championship course, from the championship tees I can shoot twenty strokes higher than I normally do. The quality of my partners' play is not what causes the change; it's the difficulty of the course. Because I want to be with the good players, and therefore play on a more difficult course, I'm out of my league. I should work my way up to that demanding course by playing lesser courses that will, over time, prepare me. By experiencing some success, I will learn faster and maintain my motivation. Recently I played a course that was so difficult that even my best was not good enough. I lost eight balls and found the experience discouraging.

Christians need to work their way toward their right level of ministry. Church leadership has the God-given responsibility to develop a system that makes progressive growth possible. People need to travel on foot before they can run with the horses. We are to climb to higher commitment, not risk disaster by leaping across dangerous chasms. The entry ports need to be many, and large directional arrows should be regularly kept in the congregational line of sight. This is done primarily through regular inspirational messages to spur them on, along with written materials that advertise entry-level opportunities. At the entry level, the opportunities should be felt-need oriented and appealing, based on contemporary community needs. But don't forget that many seekers simply want to learn about the Bible.

Building commitment requires a phased system that increases a person's commitment as he or she proceeds. A number of basic tools can make the structure work better. They are the signing of a covenant, the orientation meeting, and the integrity developed through consistency. The tools of the structure reinforce the community expectations and make people's spiritual dreams a reality.

The Covenant

Formative training in building commitment is greatly enhanced through the signing of a covenant. This teaches a person to think that joining or doing anything requires a commitment. This simple tool, rightly used, gets everyone off to a good start. I would not automatically advocate the signing of a covenant in every culture, but I do believe that where people are accustomed to signing contracts for homes and other important dealings, covenants are effective. A spiritual commitment is important, and a covenant provides a record of that commitment.

If a person resists such an action, he simply doesn't want to be on the record. Some protest that their word is good enough, and it might well be. When I buy a home I could say, "My word is good enough; we don't need a contract." We sign because it involves money, and it confirms a healthy respect for the weakness of human personality.

Why should a commitment to God not be valued as much as buying a home or renting a car? Some might say, "A commitment to God is so personal and holy that it should not be secularized through signing a piece of paper." Remember, God provided a number of important symbols to help people remember their commitments. The major feasts such as Passover, Pentecost, and others were ways to remind people of their vows to God. The building of altars such as the one in the Jordan River, to remember the crossing, were ways for the people to remember. At one time the landscape of the Holy Land was dotted with many altars. In our culture signing our names serves much the same function as an ancient altar. It is a commitment we make to God, and we do it in a public way so others can know and help.

Every agreement to a work assignment, starting with ushers, sound technicians, and greeters, should be formalized by signing a covenant that describes the purpose of the work, what they have agreed to do, and states their commitment, along with permission of those in spiritual authority over them to help them keep that commitment. Many assignments can ascend from triviality through their elevation from job to calling.

This covenant helps a person understand his or her mission. The sound technician is helping people focus on God rather than on excessive feedback; the greeter is raising the possibility that a visitor will return; the Sunday school teacher is leaving a lasting imprint on the mind and spirit of a child. This also trains the church populace to take the work of the church seriously. Only the naive claim that people naturally work as well or as hard in a volunteer setting as in one where their livelihood is on the line. People routinely think of church work as a volunteer situation, and when something is going to get squeezed out, either in time or effort, it is generally the church, because there is no immediate negative consequence, and usually the church doesn't challenge your choice, as an employer will. Part of turning around this common practice and attitude is the inauguration of a covenant system. This trains people to pray, think, count the cost, and seek counsel before they sign on for a project. It communicates the high value of faithfulness, and it treats the work of God as something highly prized. The more important a work seems, the more it will be desired by the most gifted and spiritual members of the congregation. If it is treated as unimportant, it will be considered the same. The covenant system should begin with light, short-duration commitments, and open small groups, along with work assignments mentioned above. Regardless of the assignment, entry level or elder, a covenant is essential.

The Orientation Meeting

If you don't understand the cost and the benefits, it is difficult to intelligently sign a covenant. The purpose of the orientation meeting is to fully explain the purpose, the benefits, and the requirement of the group or assignment. This brings order and thoughtfulness to the entire commitment structure. Again I cannot overstate the powerful message that is sent to the entire Christian community when this is properly practiced. The reason that orientation is not practiced is because church leaders under-appreciate its importance, are ignorant of its existence, or are too impatient to take the time. It does take more time, but in the long run it saves time, because there are fewer dropouts or restarts.

The orientation meeting requires that leaders have thought through the crucial factors of the group mission, its goals for the members, and the degree of commitment in both time and curriculum. Thus orientation lends itself to better leadership and strategic thinking.

What are some of the key factors that must make up such a meeting?

INVITE ANYONE WITH INTEREST

The invitation can be through formal means, at the church campus, or through word of mouth, based on relationship. The positive aspect of this is that many people in the church can sweep in different kinds of people without risking the integrity of the proposed group or ministry. With numerous recruiters, none are cutting deals with potential group members, a system that lends itself to the creation of various kinds of agreements that will destroy group unity and morale. Without orientation, you end up with five couples in a group who have five different understandings of the group's mission, the commitment they have made, or the desired results. The advantage of orientation is that interested parties can attend and are not already locked into the commitment. The meeting's purpose is to help people understand the commitment they would make and why the cost would be worth the benefits.

GIVE THEM THE VISION

The first and most important aspect of the orientation is to lay the vision before the potential members. One of the most crucial aspects of developing vision is relating specific activities to scriptural goals. Would-be members need to see the forest, not just individual trees. If they will be required to memorize sixty verses of Scripture, they need to see its relationship to combating sin. When outreach training is mentioned, such as using particular tools, they need to understand it as broadening their evangelistic arsenal rather than locking them into one kind of stilted outreach. Members must also understand the need to give permission to the group leader to hold them accountable as a spiritual mentor who will enhance their spiritual development.

My experience with people has been very consistent in this area. When people understand the larger purpose of specific activities, they do them with great fervor and understanding. However, if they are not regularly reminded of the larger vision for the group or assignment, the activities take on a life of their own, and people lose the vision and stop the practice of spiritual disciplines that lead to godliness.

READ THE SMALL PRINT

Many of us seem to have a "genetic" weakness that masquerades as Christian compassion. We want to make commitments sound easy. It is the silly notion that easy is more spiritual than hard. If properly prepared, I believe people aspire to higher and more demanding commitment. By making sure that everything you know about the cost is explained, those who are not willing will opt out. It is okay if some choose not to proceed because of difficulty; it will save both them and the group a great deal of heartache. If the vision doesn't overpower the cost, then so be it, and allow them to take another, less-demanding but helpful option.

One group that our church sponsored required group members to buy four tickets to our annual evangelistic

Christmas dinner; four tickets came to $100. We called it "four by faith"; this meant you would commit to the four tickets before you had anyone to bring to the dinner. The purpose of such an assignment was first to introduce people to Christ. The second was to train people to spend money on outreach. Additionally we wanted them to put their faith to the test that God would help them find someone to bring. Were there people who complained? Yes, some said it was too much; yes, some even threatened not to attend and break their commitment. But not one person could claim "bait and switch"—that we had hidden this information and then added to the original commitment. Did some people not join because of this and other requirements that had more starch in them than usual? Yes, and that's all right.

We worry too much about the fate of the less committed, when the welfare of the more committed should be of equal importance. This is in the spirit of Jesus' teaching on the cost of discipleship (Luke 9:23–25).

During orientation, tell people everything and answer their questions.

GIVE THEM TIME TO DECIDE

I am working with a number of assumptions that are treated in detail in my books *The Disciple-Making Pastor* and *The Disciple-Making Church*. Let's say there are sixty people at an orientation meeting; three groups will be started that have fourteen in a group, to bring the total to forty-two out of sixty who are expected to join. The three group leaders are trained, have been selected, and are present. After the potential members have heard all relevant information, they mark down what night of the week and what group they would like to join, if they do make the commitment. When they have left, the supervisor of those kinds of small groups meets with the new group leaders. The supervisor has led this type of group and will be responsible to give leadership to the new groups. They take the names of all sixty people, divide them into groups by interest, availability, and other factors. After one week has passed, the new group leaders begin calling the names they have been given in order to secure a commitment to their groups. The following week the groups begin to meet. Before the group begins, the small-group leader's first obligation is to secure the written covenant signed by the person or couple.

This procedure works for any kind of activity that requires a thoughtful commitment on the part of people. It is rooted in the belief that you will get a better and higher commitment. Leaders should even explain, "This is a step up, and it will cost you more, but the cost of not going on will be higher than going on."

Integrity through Consistency

This entire system will crumble like a house of cards if it loses its integrity. You can win against all objections if you are clear on expectations and exceptions are not made. People respect objectivity and fairness; if they don't, then different problems are present. When the "good ole boy" system is discarded, the fair, objective way for people to earn their spiritual wings must have integrity (1 Tim. 5:16–17). Churches are notorious for lowering expectations and becoming laissez-faire with structure and responsibility. This flacidity has led to the general ineptness of the church and is why the usual norm is so substandard.

Consistency, objectivity, and fairness eliminate the deleterious options so often available. Often, in the average church, people talk or buy their way into leadership or ascend to prominence without having passed requirements concerning their own spiritual development. Many church leaders who have been allowed a fast-track "sweetheart" deal reach powerful stations without the spiritual foundation to build or rely on. Frequently I have been challenged by those accustomed to powering their way to influence. My response has always been to say that our integrity is not for sale, and we cannot be intimidated into making exceptions that don't fit our agreed-on ethos. I have been accused of playing favorites, which means "you are not giving me the time and prestige I desire." I often answer that if we didn't have objective and clear standards for leadership, we would be left with nothing but favoritism and a personality contest. We might as well put swimsuits on our leaders and have them walk the runway at Atlantic City.

Step 3: Manage the Commitments

Once a commitment is made, it becomes leadership's God-given responsibility to manage it. Remember it is *their* commitment to God. Leaders do not make the commitment, even though leaders inspire and call on people to increase their commitments. The commitment of God's people is a sacred trust given to leaders to manage as good stewards. The role of the overseers, bishops, elders, and pastors is to direct the church and take care of the people (1 Thess. 5:12; 1 Tim. 3:5; Heb. 13:17; 1 Peter 5:2). What more precious treasure is there than the commitments the people have made to God? The commitment belongs to them; helping them keep it belongs to the leadership. The Hebrews passage categorically declares that leaders will give an account to God for how they manage the flock.

Along with gluttony and gossip, leaders' failure to manage commitment is one of the least-talked-about sins. Some church leaders pay more attention to administrative tasks or less-demanding leadership work. Some don't take this aspect of leadership seriously. They retreat into declaring that it is enough to teach the word or that much of the management activity I am about to mention is overkill or not necessary. I consider this lax attitude poor stewardship and a most grievous sin against God and the church. One of Scripture's most vivid calls to manage commitment is

Paul's comment to the Thessalonians: "And we urge you brothers, warn those who are idle, encourage the timid, help the weak, be patient with everyone" (1 Thess. 5:14).

Methods for Managing Commitment

Play it as it lays. There are two ways to accomplish commitment management. The first, well-intentioned, more common, and less effective approach is to take it as it comes. This does not call for a lot of planning or preventive work, outside of preaching and Bible studies. If someone gets out of line, we exhort or urge him to repent and change. If we learn of a person who is discouraged, we attempt to encourage; if someone is beaten down and in serious need of help, we prop her up and give her what she needs. Therefore, the most common approach is to work with the problems as they surface. This is not God's best, and there is a much better way.

Build a system. The preferred approach is to create systems that accomplish the triad task of urging, encouraging, and helping. Paul's exhortation calls us to help three kinds of needy people: the disorderly, the discouraged, and the spiritually disabled. The church can take the proactive direction of strategically placing the people into forms of ministry that address their needs before those needs reach crisis level. I have already written extensively on such a system.[2] Good leadership trains all members, thereby building a strong foundation for the entire church infrastructure. Add to this the step-by-step inspiration to and management of higher and higher commitment and the training of existing and future leaders in such a system, until this way of thinking and doing is second nature. A system is an organized way to meet needs and to fairly sort out the leaders from the followers and the faithful from the unfaithful.

If we love them, we will help people keep their commitments to God. We will do our very best as faithful stewards, which means we will put a plan into place that addresses all the known and predictable needs that are likely to occur. When will pastors wake up from their traditional work agenda slumber and realize that there is a better way than simply reacting to random need? It's sloppy, and it's sin. Leaders who understand and have training in helping people make and manage commitment are few indeed. I hope the following concepts will assist many in learning how.

Keep All Signed Covenants

Keep all signed covenants because you will need them. It helps you deal with early delinquents, who will need a written reminder that includes their signature. The covenant also buys you precious time to turn paper commitment into emotional and spiritual commitment. The written commitment means a great deal during the first three to five months of a group. After that, if the leader is not leading the group into love and relationship, the piece of paper will mean less and less. A signed covenant holds the group together around task until the glue of love and support takes hold. Love is the most powerful force for accountability that exists, and the sooner it is effective, the better.

Simply as a matter of course, all leaders should be in possession of covenants. On hundreds of occasions a group, a failing member, or leader has been rescued by the record of commitment. It's amazing how differently people can remember what they did or did not say—the covenant makes a flawed memory a nonissue. The most loving action a leader can take is to help people keep the commitment they have made by reminding them of it through a written record.

Keep Current

"Don't let the sun go down on your delinquent" was one of our leadership creeds as it related to helping people keep their commitments to God.

My yard has a weed problem; therefore, I have a weed problem. I have some choices in correcting the problem: One unacceptable option is to do nothing; a second is to hire someone else to do it; a third is to wait until the ground is covered and then spend a couple of days pulling weeds.

A spiritual leader gains nothing by ignoring a problem. It won't go away, and it would not be right to hire someone else to take care of it. Most leaders wait until the weeds are so high that they have a crisis, but the best method is to daily pull a couple of weeds and to regularly spray weed killer as a preventive measure. This approach is the one that we advocated for our leaders of various ministries. Not only is it more faithful to Scripture (Matt. 5:23–25), but it has many positive effects on the group (Eph. 4:26).

When group members begin to miss assignments, skip meetings, and little cracks begin to appear in their commitment, it's time to take action. Action early and often is essential, because it will save you greater trauma later. There is no virtue in waiting to see if it will get worse, because if you do nothing, the problem will.

Let's say that a man has been extra busy at work, and for two weeks in a row he has not done his Bible-study lesson. During the week, the leader will discuss this with his supervisor at the leadership community. He will be instructed not to be heavy-handed or judgmental, but rather to approach the person as a helper. Additionally it would be wrong to point this out in front of other members. Even if the person confesses, which is quite common, and wants to discuss it, wisdom tells us to do it later in private. We suggest that the leader casually approach the member during dessert time and point out that he has noticed the unfinished lesson. At this crucial point, seeking to be helpful, the leader asks if anything has changed recently in the person's life and if there are any special needs or pressures. It could be the man is under intense pressure and is not sleeping well or is really beaten down emotionally or physically. More commonly the person has not formed habits of Bible study and needs someone to remind him and in some cases to meet with him and help him do the lesson.

It is crucial that this delinquent Bible-study person be dealt with early for two reasons. It will be easier to get him to change in the early stages of commitment, and he will make quicker progress. Additionally the importance of group morale cannot be overemphasized. If other group members notice that standards are not maintained and that there are no consequences, you have the intolerable reality that people are being taught to disobey. *The failure must not be too important, because nothing was done,* will be the accurate conclusion of the members.

Very little is more demoralizing to a community of people than allowing some to break agreements and suffer no consequences. When people see their leaders dealing quickly and lovingly with delinquent members, it uplifts them; they know they are involved in something very special and very important. It gives them a sense of *I am doing right, and it is pleasing to God.* It also communicates how serious a commitment to God is.

The "we are all sinners and who am I to judge?" environment destroys morale. We all know we are sinners, but we are not required to accept sinful behavior as okay. God *is* the judge; we only help each other do what God has already judged. God has already pronounced his judgment against sin, and it's nothing new when we simply agree with him.

"I must ask for your forgiveness." When a leader fails himself, his charter, and his group members by not keeping current, he first must ask for their forgiveness. You may think that strange, but it conforms to the serious business of commitment. The leader made a written commitment to God, to other leaders, and to his fellow group leaders.

When he allows a person to break rank with the rest of the group and does nothing to correct it, under the delusionary belief that bad behavior left to itself will become good behavior, he has not kept his commitment to God. This approach shocks the group member who has been waiting to be confronted and who has been wondering why no one has talked to him or her. Generally one who has broken an agreement expects to be confronted about his or her behavior. It diffuses a lot of emotionally charged conversations when the leader begins by confessing his sin.

When a leader begins by saying, "First I must ask your forgiveness; I have sinned against you by not helping you keep your commitment to God. Would you forgive me?" the person will normally say yes and then add, "I need to ask for your forgiveness as well for my lack of commitment." This can be a beautiful picture of redemption, grace, and forgiveness that serves as the launching pad for even closer relationships and stronger commitment.

NO SURPRISES

There are cases when dismissal is immediate and without fanfare. As a pastor, over a period of years I made the following discoveries: A "cross dresser" was teaching our fifth-grade boys; a convicted child molester was working with junior high children; and the Sunday school superintendent was smoking pot. In those cases I had no reservations in immediately giving them their walking papers. They were relieved of their leadership responsibilities and counseled until they repented and were restored to fellowship. However, apart from similar behaviors, no one should be suddenly removed from a responsibility or group. People in the group or others with responsibilities should understand that there will be a series of warnings, clarifications, and clear communications concerning areas of concern. People should be given several chances to reform or improve, as long as they have a good attitude.

If a person is one decision away from dismissal, he should know it, and when he is dismissed, he should be the least surprised person in the kingdom.

Christian leader Dr. Henry Brandt tells a story about a store manager who, after several warnings, ignored Brandt's exhortation to manage the store rather than act like one of the sales personnel. Brandt dropped in on the store, as was his custom. On the previous trip he had told the manager that if he didn't change his pattern, he would be terminated. When Brandt entered the store, the manager was once again stocking shelves, waiting on customers, and taking part in a number of other activities that were not part of his job description. Brandt waited twenty minutes for the manager to be free. When he came over, the manager spoke about how good business was and how hard he was working. Brandt simply told the manager "You're fired." Though the manager protested, he wasn't surprised. Brandt had told him that he hadn't hired him to be a salesperson, but a manager.

Regardless of what one thinks of Brandt's action, he did not surprise the manager. No one should be surprised at a similar release from church activities.

If a person must be asked to leave a group or relinquish a responsibility, it should only follow a series of discussions and ample opportunities to make the necessary changes. However, anyone who fails to keep the commitment and won't accept help to keep it, should go. This would be true of everyone from a small-group member, group leader, elder, to the pastor. When you sit down to talk, the person should already know what is about to happen, because you have faithfully interacted over a period of time. This is one of the neglected, forgotten, or unknown pieces to pastoral care. Regular interaction is the vital link to no surprises. If that is true in your work, you have managed well.

DISMISS WITH DIGNITY

Joe was very successful in his real estate work. He was nationally known for his ability to pick good sites, arrange the funding, prepare sites for construction, and finish projects on time. What a great thing for our church to have him volunteer to give leadership to our building program! We went into our project with great confidence that his leadership would make the project a joy and a success.

Immediately, Joe realized he was in a different arena than the corporate world. Before a site could be finalized, a great deal of work needed to be done with the city to overcome some prejudices concerning church construction. Joe also learned that the church was not flush with money, like his multibillion-dollar corporation. Before we could buy, we needed a major funding campaign. The job required a great deal of flexibility; changes were required, sometimes on a daily basis. That meant several people had to be part of a decision, which meant meetings, which meant arguments, which meant time, which meant Joe didn't feel successful or in control. Additionally, Joe had little experience in being in the front lines of spiritual warfare. The enemy really didn't want us to succeed, God to be honored in the community, or the people's faith to be strengthened.

Joe committed to finish certain assignments by an agreed-on deadline. When it didn't happen, I called to find out what had happened. At first he simply said, "Oh yeah, I forgot. I'll get right on it." When there was no change, I called again. When he said, "You're not being fair. You are pressuring me," I asked to meet with him. I knew a person of his caliber and track record in the corporate world experienced a great deal of pressure. It didn't make sense that a simple pressure would affect him in this way.

At the meeting Joe shared with me that he had been depressed and would sit at home for days and do nothing with respect to our project. We talked about a number of issues, including treating his depression; he promised to move ahead, because he didn't want to let people or the Lord down. Two weeks later, the process was repeated. He was depressed, nothing was happening, and we needed to meet.

This time Joe became angry. He said I had been unfair: I changed my mind too much and he was going to expose me to the congregation.

I asked him what great evil he had to share besides the fact that the pastor changes his mind?

He responded, saying he considered that my asking him to take a look at a property other than our primary site showed a lack of integrity. He was going to expose it by addressing the congregation, resigning from his post, and exposing me for the louse I really was.

I told Joe that would force me to expose him and his failings, how he had not done what he agreed to do and that he had been depressed. Additionally I would be forced to reveal that even though he had been leading our building project, he had given no money to the church in any form during the entire preceding year.

He was aghast; he couldn't believe I would tell people those things about him.

I responded by saying, "Joe, if you are going to lie to the congregation about me, at least I can tell them the truth about you." Then I added, "There is a better way to handle this." I told him that he could save his dignity by simply resigning his position, saying that he had experienced some medical problems and that he didn't think he could give it his best. That would be true, and it would allow him to stay in the church and deal with his depression, and we could remain friends. He chose to follow my suggestion, and it did prove to be a much better solution. Joe was dismissed with dignity.

Let me be very clear on this matter. Sometimes the key to dismissing with dignity is to be faced with the prospect of losing it. At times people will threaten leadership with everything from exposure of people's private lives to lawsuits. My strong exhortation is to call their bluff. The authority of Christ in his church should not be for sale or subject to compromise. By calling their bluff, you give the threateners a way out that leaves their dignity intact. I am happy to say that the above scenario is uncommon, and hopefully you won't face it often.

A much more common form of helping people drop a commitment and maintain their dignity is when there has been a major change in their lives that interrupts their ability to keep a commitment. Serious injury, illness, or disaster need no explanation. People of common sense know that if your company transfers you there is no way to maintain a commitment. If you lose your home in a flood or experience any other kind of major life change, people are very understanding. In fact major challenges such as those mentioned can accomplish more character formation than any program.

When people drop commitments with such excuses as "I decided to go to night school," ". . . join a tennis club," ". . . work out at the club more often," or, "I just seem to stay later at the office recently," dignity becomes an issue. People who falter in their commitments over lifestyle choices should be dismissed from groups and pulled from leadership if they insist on continuing to consider those kinds of activities more crucial than their commitment to God. They should be allowed to drop, with the prospect of reentry to other future commitments. By not shaming them or insisting on making an example of them, you give them a chance to return to higher commitment when they come to their senses and see the futility of their ways. Give them an opening and tell them to run for daylight. Make sure, however, you have been truthful with them, and take this route only after they are determined to drop the commitment.

Typical Encounters of the Spiritual Kind

Why have *any* encounters or confrontations? Wouldn't it be more pleasant and civil the other way? It would be easier, but only temporary relief is possible by avoiding crucial issues. The more important question is, What would you rather have, a nonconfrontational environment where people are not keeping their commitments to God, or a confront-when-necessary environment in which a higher percentage of people keep their commitments to God? The first option will bring minor temporary relief, followed by the major misery of a weak church filled with undisciplined Christians and a disobedient leadership. The second will bring temporary discomfort and confrontations, followed by a strong, disciplined congregation that reaps a great harvest. Their leaders have been faithful and obedient because they have taken seriously their calling to help people keep their commitments to God.

Again the word *confrontation* does not require a negative emotional response from you, the reader, or the person you talk to. It simply means to deal with an issue that stands in the way of achieving a goal. It would be unloving not to help people keep the commitments they have already made. Part of making a commitment is choosing to allow another person to help you.

THE LOVING THING TO DO

For a moment we return to the needs of those who are spiritually disorderly, discouraged, and disabled (1 Thess. 5:14). The disorderly need a rebuke; the discouraged need encouragement; and the disabled need someone to pick them up and carry their burdens. These loving acts require someone to take the lead in talking with them. Generally, by becoming part of the Christian community, these people have extended permission to others to get into their lives.

Helping people obey God and overcome debilitating behavior is just as loving as when a physician removes a cancerous growth and restores a body to health. I often find it interesting how sick people will revere medical doctors who use painful treatments to solve a great problem. But the same people turn around and castigate a counselor or clergyperson for doing the same. A medical doctor can poke around on a person, creating a great deal of discomfort, until the problem is discovered. After painful surgery and other medical strategies are successful, we profusely thank the doctor. When a pastor begins to point out sinful behavior and the steps to recovery, he is often called unloving and is under siege by friends and family.

The writer to the Hebrews points out the existence of sins that give us special trouble. "Let us throw off everything that hinders and the sin that so easily entangles" (Heb. 12:1). We all have the sins that easily entangle us. Other temptations may not make us struggle as much. Some sins have blocked many a Christian from any meaningful progress. Gluttony, gossip, or a critical spirit, along with a lack of self-control, have kept well-intentioned Christians imprisoned, unable to escape on their own. This is where loving friends come to the rescue. They enter our lives and no longer let us camouflage the real reasons for our failures. They help us throw off these debilitating weights and allow us to run free of these burdens.

THE NATURE OF HUMAN NATURE

Jeremiah told us the nature of human nature is self-deceiving: "The heart is deceitful above all things and beyond cure. Who can understand it? 'I the Lord search the heart and examine the mind, to reward a man according to his conduct, according to what his deeds deserve'" (Jer. 17:9–10). *Deceit* means "to conceal the truth in order to mislead." That the heart is deceitful above all things indicates that deceit may be the inner person's primary and most natural tendency. That's why the age-old advice to follow your heart is some of the worst counsel known to humankind. For we Christians are to follow what God says is right, regardless of the inclinations or musing of our hearts.

When people clearly break with Scripture, they should be lovingly talked to by those in close relationship to them—those to whom they have given the privilege to enter into their lives. We must acknowledge that when the inclinations of our hearts conflict with the teaching of Scripture, our hearts deceive us and conceal the truth from us. That is why Scripture presents itself as giving people the direction they need to follow, rebuking us when we are wrong, and giving us the corrective action required, followed by repetition of the proper behavior that leads to righteousness (2 Tim. 3:16–17). The importance of proximity to people, so leaders can engage in meaningful dialogue with members, is essential. Helping people keep their commitments to God is a simple acknowledgment of our tendency to self-deception.

What Do You Say?

There are three primary questions to ask a person who has made a commitment and is not keeping it. But before discussing those three questions, let's cover a necessary prerequisite to success.

The assumption is that the person (or sometimes a married couple) has made a commitment to a group or task. The crucial prerequisite is to know if they want to correct the problem. Are they open to counsel? Proverbs tell us: "A rebuke impresses a man of discernment more than a hundred lashes a fool" (17:10). "Whoever corrects a mocker invites insult; whoever rebukes a wicked man incurs abuse. Do not rebuke a mocker or he will hate you; rebuke a wise man and he will love you" (9:7–8).

The people who respond to your loving interaction are wise, and eventually they will love you. If people insult and abuse you, reporting slanderous statements to their friends, they are fools. Meaningful confrontation will flush out the fools from among you and do the church and all its members a big service by their identification. If people become unreasonable and abusive, the key is to understand that future talks in good faith will only do more harm. "Do not answer a fool according to his folly, or you will be like him yourself. Answer a fool according to his folly, or he will be wise in his own eyes" (Prov. 26:4–5). This apparent contradictory proverb is clear when you think of it as advice not to act like a fool when you do answer him. If a person makes a slanderous charge, like, "You are a lying thief, and you are not a Christian." Don't yell back, "You're an ugly, stupid idiot, studying to be a moron." But if accused, you must answer in a reasoned and proper way, or some will believe what the fool has said.

Know who you are talking to and let the accuser's response become your guide as to the next course of action. If you receive a foolish reply, don't lower yourself to that person's level, but answer in a proper and orderly way. If the person is open, then treat him as someone who is wise and spiritual and who wants to work things out.

Now for the three questions for those who have failed to keep a commitment.

What Did We Agree To?

Since the commitment is in writing, everyone already knows the general answer. The issues are usually the more specific events that have arisen during participation in the group or task. Your commitment breaker may respond with, "I've developed a troubled relationship with others." "I found it harder than I first thought." "I discovered that it took more time than I expected." "I decided it wasn't what I thought." "I don't sense any progress." Or a hundred other excuses. This can be a serious problem when covenants have not been signed.

Keeping all signed covenants is essential, because there is a written record of the agreement. One evening I was in my save-a-group mode as I went to a struggling training group. I came armed with my three "killer questions," from which no one can escape.

The members complained of the memory work, the requirement to give their testimony to an unbeliever, and having to learn to do word studies in the Bible. I listened, just waiting to insert my first question.

Confidently I asked, "What did you agree to do when you signed the covenant?" Then I pulled out my copy of what they signed.

They looked startled. Then one spoke for the others, "We've never seen that document."

I looked at the leader, who was now seeking a way to slip under the carpet, for he knew he had failed to discharge his first duty as a leader: to have them sign the covenant. Suddenly, we were without common ground for any problem solving and could not return to the prescribed objective and practices of the group. This opened up endless philosophical discussions that would prove to be fruitless and serve as an excuse system. The only person I could deal with on common ground was the group leader, and I needed to wait for a private moment to do that.

The group didn't know their objective, except for that of "catchall" fellowship. They had different, and in some cases competing, agendas, and some had self-defeating agendas. They wanted to stay together, of course, because their one value was to—right or wrong—stick together. I had no choice other than to demote them by taking away the name we gave groups with their design. They accepted the change and the generic label "Bible study."

When you don't have the covenant, you can't even ask the question, "What did we agree to do?" There is no written record, and we all possess selective memories that conveniently deliver us from guilt or discipline.

It is much more common for a person to argue the interpretation of the covenant or claim there were matters not covered. The first objective of the talk is to establish common ground. If group members declare the paper invalid or go off on some emotional tangent, they have decided not to be accountable, and the decision to dismiss them from the group or responsibility is made for you.

At least half the time the problem can be solved. Most people really are new to commitment and even newer at being held to it. They sometimes "test the waters," because they are unsure that leaders will follow through. Once it has been established that this indeed was what was agreed to, you can go on to our second question.

What Has Changed?

The late Steve Holbrook, an excellent management consultant, startled me with the dogmatic declaration, "The cause of every problem is change." I challenged this statement with a variety of examples, and he easily shot them down. If you trip on the sidewalk, either the sidewalk changed or your step changed, but something changed. Today I am a firm believer in this axiom, so I ask the person who is considering dropping a commitment to God, "What has changed since you first made the commitment?" Most often a work-related change such as travel commitments or longer working hours put the squeeze on his or her schedule. Sometimes it was a broken relationship or problems with the children or a sudden illness of an older family member. The most common, however, are problems with group assignments or difficult hurdles that need to be cleared.

Many people have run from challenges all their lives. They want to experience victory over problems or difficult work assignments, but they simply "bail out." Some have a corrupted theology that says, "If it's hard and you have to keep trying over and over, then it must not be of God." How anyone can read the Bible and reach a silly belief like that is a real mystery. What people need and have needed for a long time is someone to extend a hand to help them break through this barrier of fear. Hopefully the group leader or supervisor can simply encourage them and give them hands-on help in winning over the fear.

The most challenging form of what has changed is when they accuse the leadership of "bait and switch." This term relates to the practice of selling a product to a person, and after the commitment is made, revealing a hidden cost or other information that would have killed the original sale. I first point out that "bait and switch" includes intent to deceive, and since there was no intention to deceive, the accusation is unfounded. Then I ask complainers if, when they made their marriage vows, they knew everything that would happen over a twenty-year period—or even the first year? They immediately catch the point; there is a great deal that is unknown when we enter marriage, yet it is our deepest and longest commitment. I didn't know 90 percent of what I would face as a husband, then as a father, or as a son-in-law. As long as a couple keeps their core vows of faithfulness, nurture, and love, the other issues can be managed. We don't drop our marriages just because others do or because it gets hard.

It is not uncommon for people to claim that there was not truth in advertising, in that they are not getting out of a group what was promised. Once again this usually is a vision problem joined to a theological flaw. They want maturity and responsibility now, and they want it without work. This double dip of spiritual swill can be addressed in this context, if the leader can recognize it and help people free themselves from its delusionary power. First the truth will make you miserable, then it will set you free. That spin on John 8:32 explains the principle, along with the first reaction most people have to it.

The core reasons for the commitment require review, then renewal. Once their original vision is restored, the people who want growth and Christian adventure bounce back and do very well. They simply lost their vision and forgot why they had started in the first place. Remember, when people struggle with their well-intentioned commitments, something has changed.

Are You Unwilling or Unable?

The rule of thumb is that if people are unwilling to keep their commitments, it is a spiritual issue. If they are unable, it becomes a managerial issue.

There are two kinds of unwillingness. *The first is a belligerent attitude* that says, "I'm not going to do this, it's over, and I will hold my ground." One person refused to sign a covenant once she attended the first meeting. She had given a verbal commitment, but every group member was required to sign the covenant, and all did except this person. She dug in her heels and refused to even consider signing. This was such a strong reaction that I asked if there was something in her past that would cause such a response. The question only made matters worse, and she was denied entry into the group. This level of rebellion, for no good reason other than "you can't pollute my commitment to God with such a worldly method," revealed a spiritual rebellion of substantial depth. Such unwillingness is easy to identify, and the sooner you act, the better for everyone, including the offender.

The second kind of unwillingness is a combination of fear and honest disagreement. There is room for negotiation within a particular framework, and a reasonable compromise should be sought. One of our groups' stiffer requirements was to spend money on evangelistic events. Periodically group members would be asked to spend money in advance, to cover the costs of a particular outreach. When this happened, it would be with the risk that they would not be able to get enough people there and they would lose their money. Additionally some couples claimed not to have the money in the first place. We compromised by starting a special fund for those who needed the help and discreetly helping them. Another solution was to have older group members, in their peak earning years, pay for child care for younger couples, who had less income. The unwilling spirit was changed when we found solutions.

Another dimension is fear and the power of debilitating sins in people's lives. Unwillingness to share one's faith or to learn outreach techniques were often solved by honest and caring discussion with group members. If the leader spent extra time and demonstrated certain skills for the learners, they were more willing to stay true to the commitment. The key thought is that you can't allow the disobedient to dictate to your ministry or group. Protect your groups and ministries from the truly unwilling.

The unable, on the other hand, are those who for a variety of reasons cannot, or believe they cannot, continue. This is not a spiritual issue, and thus, while no less disappointing, when they drop out, at least there isn't the negative emotional charge. One couple thought, when they separated, that they would be unable to continue in the same small group. We felt that if they would submit to counseling and work on the marriage, they could both continue. They consented to our proposal, and now, ten years later, are doing well in their marriage.

Some need to move; others have a dramatic job change. Illness disrupts the flow of life, and many other events occur over which there is very little control. In these cases we like to release people with a positive taste in their spirits. We also seek to make it possible for them to feel good about it and be able to reenter later. There are those who think they are unable and those who truly are unable. If a person starts traveling half the time and is already in the group, we find that there are ways to continue. The member may do assignments during the travel and meet with the group leader at other times. This also assumes the person is faithful when in town. Remember, the objective of all these activities is to help people keep their commitments to God and to maintain the integrity, along with the group morale, of the ministries and groups of which they are members. The infrastructure must reinforce the values of the community ethos and the definition of what it means to be a normal Christian.

I find it curious when a leader claims to practice accountability with standards and consequences, yet says he has never had to dismiss anyone. That is proof positive that he may have standards, but he is not enforcing them. If you work with real people and are faithful to the standards, there will be the need to gracefully dismiss people from ministry and groups. To question the effectiveness of dismissal is to be so pragmatic that you become impractical. There is virtue in church discipline, even when the person is not reclaimed. You have done a very important service: You have obeyed God; you have maintained the integrity of your church and your word as a leader. If your word is not built on God's Word and both are not kept, you lose the integrity of your mission.

I recall one of our high-commitment groups that started with seven couples and finished two years later with two couples. The others dropped for a variety of reasons, but they all failed to continue their commitments and were dismissed against their wills and the larger group will. So some quit because others were dismissed; they took up the other people's offense. In this group's case, the people should have been dismissed, and the two couples who finished proved to be some of the strongest Christian leaders I know. I would exchange two new, strong leadership couples for four lukewarm couples any day. That needs very little deliberation. I was not willing to allow the disobedient to set the agenda, or the semiobedient to sideline those who wanted to charge ahead. That is what it means to manage commitment.

Do you want to really love people? Help them keep their commitments to God!

Notes

Chapter 1   What Makes It So Difficult

1. Bill Hybels, "Preaching for Commitment," *Leadership Journal* 10, no. 3 (summer 1989): 350.

Chapter 3   Three Myths about Commitment

1. The full study is found in John Robinson, "Time to Work," *American Demographics* (April 1989): 68.

Chapter 4   The Top Ten Enemies of Building High Commitment

1. C. S. Lewis, "The Joyful Christian" in Ruben Job and Norman Shawchuck, *A Guide to Prayer for Ministers and Other Servants* (Nashville: The Upper Room, 1993), 320.

2. *Leadership* (spring 1994), 129.

3. Ibid.

Chapter 5   People Need Big Reasons

1. Dallas Willard, *Devotional Classics, Selected Readings for Individuals and Groups,* ed. Richard J. Foster and James Bryan Smith. A Renovare Resource for Spiritual Renewal (San Francisco: Harper & Row, 1991), 16.

Chapter 6   Ten Disciplines of the Committed Christian

1. Dallas Willard, *The Spirit of the Disciplines* (San Francisco: Harper & Row, 1988), 158–59.

2. C. H. Spurgeon, "Peace by Believing," *Metropolitan Tabernacle Pulpit* (London: Passmore and Alabaster, 1984). Reprint, vol. 9 (Pasadena, Tex.: Pilgrim Publications, 1970), 283.

3. J. I. Packer, "Foreword," in R. C. Sproul, *Knowing Scripture* (Downers Grove, Ill.: InterVarsity Press, 1979), 9–10.

4. Urban T. Holmes III, "Spirituality for Ministry" in Job and Shawchuck, *A Guide to Prayer*, 320.

5. Evelyn Underhill in Job and Shawchuck, *A Guide to Prayer*, 320.

Chapter 8   Seven Steps That Build High Commitment

1. See Bill Hull, *The Disciple-Making Church* (Grand Rapids: Fleming H. Revell, 1990).

Chapter 9   Three Steps That Maintain Commitment

1. For detailed instructions, see Hull, *The Disciple-Making Church*.

2. See Bill Hull, "The Pastor As Coach" in *The Disciple-Making Pastor* (Grand Rapids: Fleming H. Revell, 1988); and Hull, Appendix I and Appendix II in *The Disciple-Making Church*.

Bill Hull's passion is to help return the church to its disciple-making roots. This God-given desire has manifested itself with sixteen years of pastoral work and the publication of seven books. He is best known for his trilogy: *Jesus Christ, Disciple Maker, The Disciple-Making Pastor,* and *The Disciple-Making Church,* which has provided the church with a new paradigm for disciple-making. His most recent works, *Can We Save the Evangelical Church?* and *Building High Commitment in a Low-Commitment World,* are attempts to meet the pressing needs of local church leaders.